bread

...made simple

This edition published in 2012
LOVE FOOD is an imprint of Parragon Books Ltd

Parragon
Queen Street House
4 Queen Street
Bath BA1 1HE, UK

ISBN: 978-1-4454-9957-4

Printed in China

Produced by Ivy Contract
Cover and new internal photography by Clive Bozzard-Hill
Cover and new home economy by Christine France

Notes for the Reader

This book uses standard kitchen measuring spoons and cups. All spoon and cup measurements are level unless otherwise indicated. Unless otherwise stated, milk is assumed to be whole, butter is assumed to be salted, eggs are large, individual vegetables are medium, and pepper is freshly ground black pepper. Unless otherwise stated, all root vegetables should be washed and peeled before using.

For the best results, use a food thermometer when cooking meat and poultry—check the latest USDA government guidelines for current advice.

Garnishes and serving suggestions are all optional and not necessarily included in the recipe ingredients or method.

The times given are only an approximate guide. Preparation times differ according to the techniques used by different people and the cooking times may also vary from those given. Optional ingredients, variations, or serving suggestions have not been included in the calculations.

Recipes using raw or very lightly cooked eggs should be avoided by infants, the elderly, pregnant women, and people with weakened immune systems. Pregnant and breast-feeding women are advised to avoid eating peanuts and peanut products. People with nut allergies should be aware that some of the prepared ingredients used in the recipes in this book may contain nuts. Always check the packaging before use.

Picture Acknowledgments
The publisher would like to thank the following for permission to reproduce copyright material on the front cover:
Parmesan Cheese Bread © Kelly Cline/Getty images

bread

introduction

There is little to beat the satisfaction of making your own bread, creating a delectable masterpiece from a bowlful of unpromising ingredients. Kneading dough is a fabulous stress buster, and making your own bread is a genuinely pleasurable activity with the bonus of delicious, edible results. Baking bread is also a sociable experience—family and friends will crowd into the kitchen, drawn by the enticing aroma or the thought of bringing traditional favorites to life. And there is something truly wonderful about the way freshly baked bread smells, the crunch of the crust, and its warm, soft texture.

Bread is cheap to make, and a lot simpler than many people think. The basic skills required for making bread are easy to learn, and you need little in the way of specialty equipment beyond a sifter, wooden spoon, large mixing bowl, loaf pans, baking sheets, and a wire rack. And although several hours may elapse between starting and finishing the process, for a lot of that time you can do other things.

 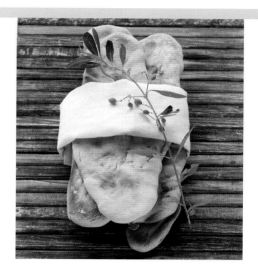

These 100 recipes feature an enticing selection of breads, from the humble white loaf to multiseed concoctions and exotic variations from all over the world. There are chapters on savory breads, for dinner and lunchtime, and dessert breads. You will also find a selection of gluten-free breads that are sure to become family favorites. Just add some chopped nuts, seeds, dried fruit, or cheese and the recipes listed here can multiply into endless mouthwatering variations. The sheer variety of styles and flavors you can use when making bread will allow you to easily create something delightful for every taste.

With a little practice, a novice bread maker can quickly gain confidence and be inspired to bake delicious and unusual breads. The results will enchant friends and family alike. From recipes for wholesome whole-wheat loaves to flatbreads, focaccias, and French baguettes, you will find plenty of inspiration on the following pages to create great bread for any occasion.

basic breads & rolls

crusty white bread

ingredients

makes 1 loaf

1 egg
1 egg yolk
²⁄₃–1 cup lukewarm water
3²⁄₃ cups white bread flour,
    plus extra for dusting
1½ teaspoons salt
2 teaspoons sugar
1 teaspoon active dry yeast
2 tablespoons butter, diced
sunflower oil, for brushing

method

1 Place the egg and egg yolk in a liquid measuring cup and beat lightly to mix. Add enough lukewarm water to make up to 1¼ cups. Stir well.

2 Sift the flour into a bowl and stir in the salt, sugar, and yeast. Add the butter and rub it in with your fingertips until the mixture resembles bread crumbs. Make a well in the center, add the egg mixture, and work to a smooth dough.

3 Invert onto a lightly floured surface and knead well for about 10 minutes, or until smooth. Brush a bowl with oil. Place the dough in the bowl and cover with a damp dish towel. Let rise in a warm place for 1 hour, or until doubled in size.

4 Brush a 9-inch loaf pan with oil. Invert the dough onto a lightly floured surface and knead for 1 minute, or until smooth. Shape the dough the length of the pan and three times the width. Fold the dough in three lengthwise and place it in the pan with the seam underneath. Cover with a dish towel and let rest in a warm place for 30 minutes, or until it has risen above the pan. Meanwhile, preheat the oven to 425°F. Place in the preheated oven and bake for 30 minutes, or until firm and golden brown. Transfer to a wire rack to cool.

whole-wheat harvest bread

ingredients

makes 1 loaf

8 ounces whole-wheat bread flour,
  plus extra for dusting
1 tablespoon instant nonfat
  dry milk
1 teaspoon salt
2 tablespoons packed light
  brown sugar
1 teaspoon active dry yeast
1½ tablespoons sunflower oil,
  plus extra for brushing
¾ cup lukewarm water
butter, to serve

method

1 Put the flour, instant dry milk, salt, sugar, and yeast into a bowl. Make a well in the center, pour in the oil, and add the water, then mix well to make a smooth dough.

2 Invert onto a lightly floured surface and knead well for about 10 minutes, or until smooth. Brush a bowl with oil. Shape the dough into a ball, place it in the bowl, and cover with a damp dish towel. Let rise in a warm place for 1 hour, or until doubled in size.

3 Brush a 9-inch loaf pan with oil. Invert the dough onto a lightly floured surface and knead for 1 minute, or until smooth. Shape the dough to the length of the pan and three times the width. Fold the dough into three lengthwise and place it in the pan with the seam underneath. Cover and let rest in a warm place for 30 minutes, or until it has risen above the pan. Meanwhile, preheat the oven to 425°F.

4 Place the bread in the preheated oven and bake for 30 minutes, or until firm and golden brown. Transfer to a wire rack to cool. Serve with butter.

multigrain bread

ingredients

makes 1 loaf

2⅔ cups multigrain bread flour, plus extra for dusting
1 tablespoon olive oil, plus extra for brushing
1½ teaspoons salt
1 envelope active dry yeast
1 tablespoon honey
1 cup warm water

method

1 Put the flour into a bowl and stir in the oil, salt, and yeast. Make a well in the center, add the honey to the water, pour into the flour mixture, and mix to form a soft dough. If it is sticky, add a little more flour.

2 Invert the dough onto a lightly floured surface and knead for 10 minutes.

3 Return the dough to the mixing bowl and cover with lightly oiled plastic wrap. Let rest in a warm place for about 1½ hours, or until doubled in size.

4 Invert the dough and knead again gently for 1 minute. Brush a 9-inch loaf pan with oil. Put the dough in the pan, cover, and let rest in a warm place to rise again for about 30 minutes. Meanwhile, preheat the oven to 400°F.

5 Bake the loaf for 35–40 minutes, or until firm and golden brown. Transfer to a wire rack to cool.

quick whole-wheat loaf

ingredients

makes 1 loaf

1 envelope active dry yeast
1 teaspoon sugar
1¾ cups lukewarm water
3⅔ cups whole-wheat bread flour
1 teaspoon salt
oil, for brushing

method

1 Stir the yeast and sugar into ½ cup of the water, then let stand for about 10 minutes, or until frothy.

2 Put the flour into a bowl and stir in the salt. Make a well in the center and add the yeast mixture and remaining water, mixing thoroughly to a soft dough.

3 Brush a 9-inch loaf pan with oil. Transfer the dough into the prepared pan and place the pan in a large plastic food bag. Let rise in a warm place for about 1 hour, or until the dough reaches the top of the pan. Meanwhile, preheat the oven to 400°F.

4 Bake the loaf in the preheated oven for 30–35 minutes, or until firm and golden brown. Transfer to a wire rack to cool.

half & half loaf

ingredients

makes 1 loaf

2½ cups white bread flour,
  plus extra for dusting
1¼ cups whole-wheat bread flour
1 envelope active dry yeast
1½ teaspoons salt
1½ cups lukewarm water
2 tablespoons olive oil
vegetable oil, for brushing

method

1 Sift 2 cups of the white flour into a bowl, and mix the remainder with the whole-wheat flour in a separate bowl. Add half the yeast and half the salt to each bowl.

2 Make a well in the center of each flour mix and add about half the water and oil to each bowl, mixing to a soft dough. The two mixtures should be about the same consistency.

3 Invert the doughs onto a lightly floured surface and knead separately for 10 minutes, or until smooth. Return the doughs to the separate mixing bowls. Cover and let rest for 5 minutes.

4 Brush a 9-inch loaf pan with oil. Invert the doughs, shape each into a smooth circle, and place one circle in each end of the prepared pan. Cover and let rest in a warm place for about 1 hour, or until risen just above the top of the pan. Meanwhile, preheat the oven to 450°F.

5 Bake the loaf in the preheated oven for 5 minutes, then reduce the oven temperature to 400°F and bake for an additional 25–30 minutes, or until firm and golden brown. Transfer to a wire rack to cool.

mixed seed bread

ingredients

makes 1 loaf

2¾ cups white bread flour, plus extra for dusting

1¼ cups rye flour

1½ teaspoons salt

1½ tablespoons instant nonfat dry milk

1 tablespoon packed light brown sugar

1 teaspoon active dry yeast

1½ tablespoons sunflower oil, plus extra for brushing

2 teaspoons lemon juice

1¼ cups lukewarm water

1 teaspoon caraway seeds

½ teaspoon poppy seeds

½ teaspoon sesame seeds

topping

1 egg white

1 tablespoon water

1 tablespoon sunflower seeds or pumpkin seeds

method

1 Put the flours into a bowl and stir in the salt, instant dry milk, sugar, and yeast. Pour in the oil and add the lemon juice and water. Stir in the seeds and mix well to make a smooth dough. Invert onto a lightly floured surface and knead well for about 10 minutes, or until smooth and elastic.

2 Brush a bowl with oil. Shape the dough into a ball, place it in the bowl, and cover with a damp dish towel. Let rise in a warm place for 1 hour, or until doubled in size.

3 Brush a 9-inch loaf pan with oil. Invert the dough onto a lightly floured surface and knead for 1 minute, or until smooth. Shape the dough to the length of the pan and three times the width. Fold the dough in three lengthwise and place it in the pan with the seam underneath. Cover with a dish towel and let rest in a warm place for 30 minutes, or until it has risen above the pan. Meanwhile, preheat the oven to 425°F.

4 For the topping, lightly beat the egg white with the water to make a glaze. Brush the glaze over the loaf, then gently press the sunflower seeds all over the top.

5 Bake in the preheated oven for 30 minutes, or until firm and golden brown. Transfer to a wire rack to cool.

seven-grain bread

ingredients

makes 1 loaf

3½ tablespoons whole-grain millet
2¼ cups whole-wheat bread flour
1¾ cups white spelt flour,
    plus extra for dusting
1 envelope active dry yeast
1½ teaspoons salt
⅓ cup rye flakes
½ cup rolled oats
⅓ cup cornmeal, plus extra
    for sprinkling
2 tablespoons sesame seeds
1½ cups lukewarm water
1 tablespoon olive oil
1 tablespoon white wine vinegar
vegetable oil, for brushing
butter, to serve

method

1 Bring a saucepan of water to the boil, add the millet, bring back to the boil, and simmer for 10 minutes. Drain well.

2 Combine the whole-wheat flour and spelt flour in a bowl and stir in the yeast and salt. Stir in the rye flakes, oats, cornmeal, cooked millet, and sesame seeds and mix well. Make a well in the center and add the water, oil, and vinegar, mixing to a soft dough.

3 Invert the dough onto a lightly floured surface and knead for about 10 minutes. Place the dough back in the mixing bowl, cover, and let rest for 5 minutes.

4 Brush a baking sheet with oil. Invert the dough and knead lightly until smooth, then shape into a large round loaf. Sprinkle the prepared baking sheet with cornmeal, place the dough on the sheet, and slash the top with a sharp knife in a crisscross pattern.

5 Cover and let rest in a warm place for about 1 hour, or until doubled in size. Meanwhile, preheat the oven to 425°F.

6 Bake in the preheated oven for 10 minutes, then reduce the oven temperature to 400°F and bake for an additional 20–25 minutes, or until firm and golden brown. Transfer to a wire rack to cool. Serve with butter.

sunflower twist

ingredients

makes 1 loaf

2¼ cups white bread flour, plus
    extra for dusting
1½ cups whole-wheat bread flour
1 envelope active dry yeast
1½ teaspoons salt
1 cup lukewarm water
½ cup apple juice
1 tablespoon sunflower oil,
    plus extra for brushing
¾ cup sunflower seeds
milk, for glazing

method

1 Sift the white flour into a bowl, add the whole-wheat flour, and stir in the yeast and salt. Make a well in the center and add the water, apple juice, and oil, mixing to a soft dough.

2 Invert the dough onto a lightly floured surface and knead for about 10 minutes. Place the dough back in the mixing bowl, cover, and let rest for 5 minutes.

3 Brush a baking sheet with oil. Invert the dough and knead in about two-thirds of the sunflower seeds. Divide the dough in half and shape each piece into a 10-inch-long log shape. Twist together the two pieces of dough, firmly pinching the ends to seal.

4 Place on the prepared baking sheet, allowing room for spreading. Cover and let rest in a warm place for about 1 hour, or until doubled in size. Meanwhile, preheat the oven to 450°F.

5 Brush the dough with milk and sprinkle with the remaining sunflower seeds. Bake in the preheated oven for 10 minutes, then reduce the oven temperature to 425°F and bake for an additional 20–25 minutes, or until firm and golden brown. Transfer to a wire rack to cool.

rye bread

ingredients

makes 1 loaf

1²/₃ cups white bread flour, plus extra for dusting

4½ cups rye flour

2 teaspoons salt

2 teaspoons packed light brown sugar

1 envelope active dry yeast

1¾ cups lukewarm water, plus 1 extra tablespoon for glazing

2 teaspoons vegetable oil, plus extra for brushing

1 egg white

method

1 Sift the white flour into a bowl, add the rye flour, and stir in the salt, sugar, and yeast. Make a well in the center and pour in the water and oil. Stir until the dough begins to come together, then knead until it leaves the side of the bowl. Invert onto a lightly floured surface and knead for 10 minutes, or until elastic and smooth. Shape the dough into a ball, put into a bowl brushed with oil, cover, and let rise in a warm place for 2 hours, or until doubled in size.

2 Brush a baking sheet with oil. Invert the dough onto a lightly floured surface and knead for 10 minutes. Shape the dough into a ball, put it on the prepared baking sheet, and cover. Let rise in a warm place for an additional 40 minutes, or until doubled in size.

3 Meanwhile, preheat the oven to 375°F. Beat the egg white with 1 tablespoon of water in a bowl. Bake the loaf in the preheated oven for 20 minutes, then remove from the oven and brush the top with the egg white glaze. Return to the oven and bake for an additional 20 minutes.

4 Remove from the oven, brush the top of the loaf with the glaze again, and return to the oven for an additional 20–30 minutes, or until the crust is a rich brown. Transfer to a wire rack to cool.

pumpernickel bread

ingredients

makes 1 loaf

1½ cups white bread flour,
   plus extra for dusting
2½ cups rye flour
1 envelope active dry yeast
1½ teaspoons salt
2 teaspoons caraway seeds
1 tablespoon molasses
1¼ cups lukewarm water
oil, for brushing
beaten egg, for glazing
cheese, to serve (optional)

method

1 Sift the white flour into a bowl, add the rye flour, stir in the yeast, salt, and caraway seeds, then make a well in the center. Dissolve the molasses in the water and stir into the dry ingredients, mixing to a soft dough.

2 Invert the dough onto a lightly floured surface and knead for about 10 minutes. Return the dough to the mixing bowl, cover, and let rest for 5 minutes.

3 Brush a baking sheet with oil. Invert the dough and knead briefly for 1 minute. Shape into an oval about 14 inches long. Place on the prepared baking sheet and slash the top diagonally at intervals with a sharp knife.

4 Cover and let rest in a warm place for about 1 hour, or until doubled in size. Meanwhile, preheat the oven to 375°F.

5 Bake the loaf in the preheated oven for 20 minutes. Mix the egg with 1 tablespoon of cold water and brush over the loaf to glaze. Reduce the oven temperature to 350°F, return the loaf to the oven, and bake for an additional 20–25 minutes, or until firm. Transfer to a wire rack to cool. Serve with cheese, if liked.

sourdough bread

ingredients

makes 2 loaves

3¾ cups whole-wheat flour
4 teaspoons salt
1½ cups lukewarm water
2 tablespoons molasses
1 tablespoon vegetable oil,
    plus extra for brushing
all-purpose flour, for dusting

starter

¾ cup whole-wheat flour
⅔ cup white bread flour
¼ cup sugar
1 cup milk

method

1 First, make the starter. Put the flours, sugar, and milk into a nonmetallic bowl and beat well with a fork. Cover with a damp dish towel and let rest in a warm place for 4–5 days, until it is frothy and smells sour. If it has a pink, orange, or other odd color, dispose of it and try again.

2 Put the flour and half the salt into a bowl and add the water, molasses, vegetable oil, and sourdough starter. Mix well with a wooden spoon until a dough begins to form, then knead with your hands until it leaves the side of the bowl. Invert onto a lightly floured surface and knead for 10 minutes, or until smooth and elastic.

3 Form the dough into a ball and put it into a bowl brushed with oil. Cover and let rise in a warm place for 2 hours, or until doubled in size. Dust two baking sheets with flour. Mix the remaining salt with ¼ cup of water in a bowl. Invert the dough onto a lightly floured surface and knead for an additional 10 minutes. Halve the dough, shape each piece into an oval, and place on the prepared baking sheets. Brush with the salt water glaze and let stand in a warm place, brushing frequently with the glaze, for 30 minutes. Preheat the oven to 425°F.

4 Brush the loaves with the remaining glaze and bake for 30 minutes, or until firm and golden brown. Transfer to wire racks to cool.

saffron finger rolls

ingredients

makes 12

1 teaspoon saffron strands
3 tablespoons boiling water
3²/₃ cups white bread flour,
   plus extra for dusting
1 envelope active dry yeast
1½ teaspoons salt
1¼ cups lukewarm milk
2 tablespoons butter, melted and
   cooled slightly
vegetable oil, for brushing

method

1 Place the saffron in a small bowl and pour the boiling water over it. Let stand for 30 minutes.

2 Sift the flour into a bowl and stir in the yeast and salt. Make a well in the center and add the milk, butter, and saffron with its liquid, mixing to a soft dough.

3 Invert the dough onto a lightly floured surface and knead for about 10 minutes, until smooth. Place the dough back in the mixing bowl, cover, and let rest for 5 minutes.

4 Brush a large baking sheet with oil. Invert the dough and lightly knead, then divide into 12 pieces and shape each into a 4-inch-long finger shape.

5 Place the rolls on the prepared baking sheet about 1 inch apart and use a sharp knife to cut a shallow lengthwise slash on top of each. Cover and let rest in a warm place for about 1 hour, or until the rolls are doubled in size and almost touching. Meanwhile, preheat the oven to 425°F.

6 Bake the rolls in the preheated oven for 15–20 minutes, or until golden brown. Transfer to a wire rack to cool.

hamburger buns

ingredients

makes 8

3⅓ cups white bread flour, plus
   extra for dusting
1½ teaspoons salt
2 teaspoons sugar
1 teaspoon active dry yeast
⅔ cup lukewarm water
⅔ cup lukewarm milk
vegetable oil, for brushing
2–3 tablespoons sesame seeds

method

1 Sift together the flour and salt into a bowl and stir in the sugar and yeast. Make a well in the center and pour in the water and milk. Stir well until the dough begins to come together, then knead until it leaves the side of the bowl. Invert onto a lightly floured surface and knead for about 10 minutes, or until smooth and elastic.

2 Brush a bowl with oil. Shape the dough into a ball, put it in the bowl, and cover. Let rise in a warm place for 1 hour, or until doubled in size.

3 Brush two baking sheets with oil. Invert the dough onto a lightly floured surface and knead briefly. Divide it into eight equal pieces, shape each into a ball, and put them on the prepared baking sheets. Flatten slightly with a lightly floured hand and cover. Let rise in a warm place for 30 minutes. Meanwhile, preheat the oven to 400°F.

4 Lightly press the center of each bun with your fingers to release any large air bubbles. Brush the tops with the oil and sprinkle with sesame seeds. Bake for 15–20 minutes, or until light golden brown. Transfer to a wire rack to cool.

parker house rolls

ingredients

makes 12

½ cup milk
¼ cup water
5 tablespoons butter, softened,
    plus extra for brushing
2½ cups white bread flour,
    plus extra for dusting
½ teaspoon salt
1 envelope active dry yeast
1 tablespoon sugar
1 extra-large egg, beaten
sunflower oil, for brushing

method

1 Put the milk, water, and half of the butter into a saucepan and heat gently until combined. Sift together the flour and salt into a bowl and stir in the yeast and sugar. Make a well in the center and slowly pour in half of the milk mixture, then mix in the egg. Slowly stir in the remaining milk mixture until a soft dough forms.

2 Brush a bowl with oil. Invert the dough onto a lightly floured surface and knead for 8–10 minutes, or until smooth and elastic. Put the dough into the bowl, cover, and set aside for 1 hour, or until doubled in size.

3 Invert the dough onto a lightly floured surface and knead for 1–2 minutes. Cover and let rest for 10 minutes. Preheat the oven to 400°F and dust a baking sheet with flour. Melt the remaining butter in a small saucepan over medium heat.

4 Roll out the dough to a thickness of ¼ inch. Stamp out 12 circles with a ¼-inch round cutter. Brush the middle of each circle with butter, fold over, and pinch together the edges to seal. Place on the prepared baking sheet.

5 Lightly brush the tops of the rolls with butter and bake in the preheated oven for 12–15 minutes, or until firm and golden brown. Transfer to a wire rack to cool.

cashew nut rolls

ingredients

makes 8

⅔ cup cashew nuts
3⅔ cups white bread flour, plus
    extra for dusting
1 envelope active dry yeast
1½ teaspoons salt
1 cup lukewarm water
½ cup lukewarm milk
vegetable oil, for brushing
beaten egg, for glazing
butter, to serve

method

1 Coarsely chop 2 tablespoons of the nuts and grind the remainder in a food processor, or finely chop.

2 Sift the flour into a bowl and stir in the yeast, salt, and ground nuts. Make a well in the center and add the water and milk, mixing to a soft dough.

3 Invert the dough onto a lightly floured surface and knead for about 10 minutes, until smooth. Place the dough back in the mixing bowl, cover, and let rest for 5 minutes.

4 Brush a baking sheet with oil. Invert the dough and lightly knead, then divide into eight pieces and shape each piece into a 10-inch-long log shape. Loosely tie each length of dough into a knot and place on the prepared baking sheet, allowing room for spreading.

5 Cover and let rest in a warm place for about 1 hour, or until doubled in size. Meanwhile, preheat the oven to 425°F.

6 Brush the rolls with the beaten egg and sprinkle with the chopped nuts. Bake in the preheated oven for 15–20 minutes, or until firm and golden brown. Transfer to a wire rack to cool. Serve with butter.

english muffins

ingredients

makes 8

3²/₃ cups white bread flour,
    plus extra for dusting
1 envelope active dry yeast
1 teaspoon salt
1 teaspoon sugar
1 cup lukewarm water
²/₃ cup plain yogurt
semolina, for sprinkling
sunflower oil, for brushing
butter and raspberry jam, to serve

method

1 Sift the flour into a bowl and stir in the yeast, salt, and sugar. Make a well in the center and add the water and yogurt, mixing to a soft dough.

2 Invert the dough onto a lightly floured surface and knead for 10 minutes, or until smooth. Place the dough back in the mixing bowl, cover, and let rest for 5 minutes.

3 Invert the dough and roll out to a thickness of about ³/₄ inch. Stamp out eight circles with a 3-inch round cutter.

4 Sprinkle a baking sheet with semolina, arrange the muffins on top, and sprinkle with more semolina. Cover and let rest in a warm place for about 1 hour, or until doubled in size.

5 Heat a flat griddle pan or heavy skillet until hot and brush with oil. Add the muffins and reduce the heat to medium, then cook in batches for about 12 minutes, turning once, or until firm and golden brown. Transfer to a wire rack to cool. Serve with butter and raspberry jam, if liked.

bagels

ingredients

makes 10

2½ cups white bread flour,
    plus extra for dusting
2 teaspoons salt
1 envelope active dry yeast
1 tablespoon lightly beaten egg
1 cup lukewarm water
vegetable oil, for brushing
butter, to serve

glaze

1 egg white
2 teaspoons water
2 tablespoons caraway seeds

method

1 Sift together the flour and salt into a bowl and stir in the yeast. Make a well in the center, pour in the egg and the water, and mix to a dough. Invert onto a lightly floured surface and knead well for about 10 minutes, or until smooth. Brush a bowl with oil. Shape the dough into a ball, place it in the bowl, and cover. Let rise for 1 hour, or until doubled in size.

2 Brush two baking sheets with oil and dust a sheet with flour. Invert the dough onto a lightly floured surface and knead for 2 minutes. Divide into ten pieces, shape each into a ball, and let rest for 5 minutes. Flatten each ball with a lightly floured hand and make a hole in the center. Put the bagels on the floured sheet, cover, and let rise for 20 minutes.

3 Meanwhile, preheat the oven to 425°F and bring a saucepan of water to a boil. Reduce the heat until the water is barely simmering, then add two bagels. Poach for 1–2 minutes, turning over in the water. Remove with a slotted spoon and drain on a dish towel. Poach the remaining bagels in the same way. Transfer the bagels to the prepared baking sheets. Beat the egg white with the water in a bowl and brush it over the bagels. Sprinkle with the caraway seeds and bake in the preheated oven for 25–30 minutes, or until golden brown. Transfer to a wire rack to cool. Serve with butter.

breadsticks

ingredients

makes 30

2½ cups white bread flour,
 plus extra for dusting
1½ teaspoons salt
1 envelope active dry yeast
1 cup lukewarm water
3 tablespoons olive oil, plus extra
 for brushing
sesame seeds, for coating

method

1 Sift together the flour and salt into a bowl. Stir in the yeast. Make a well in the center. Add the water and oil to the well and mix to form a soft dough.

2 Invert the dough onto a lightly floured work surface and knead for 5–10 minutes, or until smooth and elastic. Put the dough in an oiled bowl, cover, and let rise for 1 hour, or until doubled in size.

3 Preheat the oven to 400°F. Brush two baking sheets with oil.

4 Invert the dough again and knead lightly. Roll out into a rectangle measuring 9 x 8 inches. Cut the dough into three strips, each 8 inches long, then cut each strip across into ten equal pieces.

5 Roll and stretch each piece of dough into a stick about 12 inches long, then brush with oil. Spread out the sesame seeds on a large shallow plate or sheet. Roll each breadstick in the sesame seeds to coat, then space well apart on the prepared baking sheets. Brush with oil, cover, and let rise for 15 minutes.

6 Bake in the preheated oven for 10 minutes. Turn over and bake for an additional 5–10 minutes, or until golden. Transfer to a wire rack and let cool.

savory breads

sun-dried tomato rolls

ingredients

makes 8

1²/₃ cups white bread flour, plus extra for dusting

½ teaspoon salt

1 envelope active dry yeast

1 stick butter, melted and cooled slightly, plus extra for greasing

3 tablespoons milk, warmed

2 eggs, beaten

⅓ cup drained and finely chopped sun-dried tomatoes

milk, for brushing

method

1 Sift together the flour and salt into a bowl. Stir in the yeast, then pour in the butter, milk, and eggs. Mix together to form a dough.

2 Turn the dough onto a lightly floured work surface and knead for about 5 minutes.

3 Brush a bowl with butter. Place the dough in the bowl, cover, and let rise for 1–1½ hours, or until doubled in size.

4 Meanwhile, preheat the oven to 450°F. Lightly grease a baking sheet. Invert the dough and knead for about 2–3 minutes. Sprinkle the work surface with extra flour—the sun-dried tomatoes are oily—then knead the sun-dried tomatoes into the dough.

5 Divide the dough into eight balls and place them on the prepared baking sheet. Cover and let rise for about 30 minutes, or until the rolls have doubled in size.

6 Brush the rolls with milk and bake in the preheated oven for 10–15 minutes, or until golden brown. Transfer to a wire rack to cool.

cherry tomato, rosemary & sea salt focaccia

ingredients

makes 1 loaf

⅓ cup olive oil, plus extra
   for brushing
2 garlic cloves, crushed
2½ cups white bread flour,
   plus extra for dusting
2 teaspoons salt
1 envelope active dry yeast
1 teaspoon sugar
1 cup lukewarm water
2 teaspoons finely chopped
   fresh rosemary
12–13 ripe red cherry tomatoes
¼ teaspoon flaky sea salt

method

1 Mix together 2 tablespoons of the oil and all of the garlic. Set aside. Sift together the flour and salt in a bowl and stir in the yeast and sugar. Add the remaining oil and water. Mix to a dough. Invert onto a lightly floured surface and knead for 10 minutes, until smooth and elastic, then knead in 1 tablespoon of the garlic-flavored oil.

2 Brush a 6½ x 10-inch baking pan with oil. Press the dough over the bottom of the pan with your hands. Brush with the remaining garlic oil, then sprinkle with the rosemary. Cover loosely with plastic wrap and set aside in a warm place for about 1 hour, until puffed up and doubled in size.

3 Preheat the oven to 450°F. Place the tomatoes over the focaccia and press them into the bottom of the dough. Sprinkle with the sea salt. Place in the preheated oven and immediately reduce the temperature to 400°F. Bake for 25–30 minutes, or until firm and golden brown. Transfer to a wire rack to cool.

bruschetta with tomato, red onion & basil salsa

ingredients

serves 6

1 large baguette (see page 106)
2 tablespoons basil oil

salsa
2 red onions
½ cup fresh basil leaves
10 plum tomatoes, peeled,
    seeded, and diced
juice of 2 lemons
salt and pepper

method

1 Preheat the oven to 450°F.

2 Slice open the baguette and place on a baking sheet. Brush with some of the oil and place in the oven. Toast until golden brown.

3 Chop the onions and basil and combine with the tomatoes, lemon juice, and the remaining oil. Season with salt and pepper. Spoon the salsa over each slice of toasted bread and serve.

whole-wheat carrot rolls

ingredients

makes 8

1¾ cups white bread flour,
plus extra for dusting
1¾ cups whole-wheat bread flour,
plus extra for sprinkling
1 envelope active dry yeast
1½ teaspoons salt
1¼ cups lukewarm water
2 tablespoons olive oil
3 carrots, shredded
(about 1½ cups)
vegetable oil, for brushing

method

1 Sift the white flour into a bowl, add the whole-wheat flour, and stir in the yeast and salt. Make a well in the center and add the water, olive oil, and carrots, mixing to a soft dough.

2 Invert the dough onto a lightly floured surface and knead for about 10 minutes, until smooth. Place the dough in a bowl, cover, and let rest for 5 minutes.

3 Brush a baking sheet with oil. Invert the dough and lightly knead again until smooth. Divide into eight pieces, shape each piece into a ball, and arrange on the prepared baking sheet, allowing room for spreading.

4 Cover and let rest in a warm place for about 1 hour, or until doubled in size. Meanwhile, preheat the oven to 425°F.

5 Sprinkle the rolls with a little whole-wheat flour and bake in the preheated oven for 12–15 minutes, or until golden brown. Transfer to a wire rack to cool.

zucchini & parmesan bread

ingredients

makes 1 loaf

1¾ cups all-purpose white flour, plus extra for dusting

2 cups whole-wheat flour

1½ tablespoons baking powder

1 teaspoon salt

1½ teaspoons dry mustard

4 tablespoons butter, diced, plus extra for greasing

1 zucchini, shredded and patted dry

1⅔ cups finely grated fresh Parmesan cheese

1 teaspoon finely chopped fresh thyme

2 eggs, beaten

about ¾ cup low-fat milk

pepper

butter and cheese, to serve (optional)

method

1 Preheat the oven to 375°F. Grease a baking sheet and set aside. Put the flours into a bowl, stir in the baking powder, salt, pepper, and dry mustard, then lightly rub in the butter until the mixture resembles bread crumbs. Stir in the zucchini, Parmesan cheese, and chopped thyme. Stir in the eggs and enough milk to form a soft dough.

2 Invert the dough onto a lightly floured surface and knead lightly, then shape into an 8-inch circle. Place on the prepared baking sheet, then cut three fairly deep slashes in the top of the loaf using a sharp knife.

3 Bake in the preheated oven for 40–50 minutes, or until well risen and deep golden brown. Transfer to a wire rack to cool. Serve warm or cold in slices, on its own, with cheese or spread with butter.

variation

Replace the Parmesan cheese with 1 cup freshly cooked, chopped cremini mushrooms and substitute 2 tablespoons of chopped fresh basil for the thyme.

walnut & seed bread

ingredients

makes 2 large loaves

3¾ cups whole-wheat flour
3¾ cups multigrain flour
¾ cup white bread flour,
    plus extra for dusting
2 tablespoons sesame seeds
2 tablespoons sunflower seeds
2 tablespoons poppy seeds
1 cup chopped walnuts
2 teaspoons salt
2 envelopes active dry yeast
2 tablespoons olive oil or
    walnut oil
3 cups lukewarm water
1 tablespoon butter, melted, or oil,
    for greasing

method

1 Put the flours, seeds, walnuts, salt, and yeast into a bowl and mix together. Make a well in the center, add the oil and water, and stir well to form a soft dough. Invert the dough onto a lightly floured surface and knead well for 5–7 minutes, or until smooth and elastic.

2 Return the dough to the bowl, cover with a damp dish towel, and let rest in a warm place for 1–1½ hours to rise, or until doubled in size. Invert onto a lightly floured surface and knead again for 1 minute.

3 Brush two 9-inch loaf pans well with the melted butter or oil. Divide the dough in two. Shape one piece the length of the pan and three times the width. Fold the dough in three lengthwise and place in one of the pans with the seam underneath. Repeat with the other piece of dough.

4 Cover and let rise again in a warm place for about 30 minutes, or until well risen above the pans. Meanwhile, preheat the oven to 450°F.

5 Bake the loaves in the center of the preheated oven for 25–30 minutes. If the loaves are getting too brown, reduce the temperature to 425°F. Transfer to wire racks to cool.

caramelized onion baguettes

ingredients

makes 3 small baguettes

2 tablespoons olive oil
1 large onion, thinly sliced
1 garlic clove, thinly sliced
1 tablespoon balsamic vinegar
3⅔ cups white bread flour,
    plus extra for dusting
1 envelope active dry yeast
2 teaspoons salt
1¼ cups lukewarm water
1 tablespoon honey
vegetable oil, for brushing

method

1 Heat the olive oil in a small skillet, add the onion and garlic, and sauté for 8–10 minutes, stirring continuously, or until soft. Stir in the balsamic vinegar, then transfer the mixture to a bowl and let cool slightly.

2 Sift the flour into a bowl and stir in the yeast and salt. Make a well in the center and add the water and honey. Stir in the onion mixture and knead to a soft, sticky dough.

3 Invert the dough onto a lightly floured surface and knead for about 10 minutes, or until evenly mixed and elastic. Cover and let rest for 5 minutes.

4 Brush a baking sheet with oil. Divide the dough into three pieces, shape each piece into a ball, then roll with your hands to form 12-inch-long baguette shapes. Place the baguettes on the prepared baking sheet. Slash the tops of the baguettes four to five times with a sharp knife. Cover and let rest in a warm place for about 1 hour, or until doubled in size. Meanwhile, preheat the oven to 450°F.

5 Spray the preheated oven with water, then place the baguettes in the oven and spray the oven again. Bake for 12–15 minutes, or until golden brown. Transfer to a wire rack to cool.

flatbread with onion & rosemary

ingredients

makes 1 loaf

3¼ cups white bread flour, plus extra for dusting
½ teaspoon salt
1 envelope active dry yeast
2 tablespoons chopped fresh rosemary, plus small sprigs to garnish
⅓ cup extra virgin olive oil, plus extra for brushing
1¼ cups lukewarm water
1 red onion, thinly sliced and pushed out into rings
1 tablespoon coarse sea salt

method

1 Sift together the flour and salt into a bowl and stir in the yeast and rosemary. Make a well in the center and pour in 3 tablespoons of the olive oil and the water. Stir well until the dough begins to come together, then knead until it leaves the side of the bowl. Invert onto a lightly floured surface and knead well for about 10 minutes, or until smooth and elastic.

2 Brush a bowl with oil. Shape the dough into a ball, put it in the bowl, and cover with a damp dish towel. Let rise in a warm place for 1 hour, or until doubled in size.

3 Brush a baking sheet with oil. Invert the dough onto a lightly floured surface and knead for 1 minute. Roll out the dough to a circle about 12 inches in diameter and put it on the prepared baking sheet. Cover and let the dough rise in a warm place for 20–30 minutes.

4 Preheat the oven to 400°F. Using the handle of a wooden spoon, make indentations all over the surface of the loaf. Spread the onion rings over the top, drizzle with the remaining oil, and sprinkle with the sea salt. Bake for 20 minutes. Sprinkle with the rosemary sprigs, return to the oven, and bake for an additional 5 minutes, or until golden brown. Transfer to a wire rack to cool slightly and serve warm.

garlic bread rolls

ingredients

makes 8

butter, for greasing
12 garlic cloves
1½ cups milk
3¼ cups white bread flour
1 teaspoon salt
1 envelope active dry yeast
1 tablespoon dried mixed herbs,
    such as oregano, thyme,
    and/or rosemary
3 tablespoons sunflower oil
1 egg, lightly beaten
milk, for brushing
sea salt, for sprinkling

method

1 Grease a baking sheet with a little butter and set aside. Place the garlic cloves and milk in a saucepan, bring to a boil, and simmer gently for 15 minutes. Cool slightly, then process in a food processor or blender to blend in the garlic.

2 Sift together the flour and salt into a bowl, stir in the yeast, then add the mixed herbs. Add the garlic-flavored milk, sunflower oil, and beaten egg to the dry ingredients and mix to form a dough.

3 Place the dough on a lightly floured work surface and knead gently for a few minutes until smooth and soft.

4 Grease a bowl with butter. Place the dough in the bowl, cover, and let rise in a warm place for about 1 hour, or until doubled in size.

5 Knead the dough for 2 minutes. Divide the dough into eight pieces and shape into rolls. Score the tops of the rolls with a knife and place them on the prepared baking sheet. Cover and let rest for 15 minutes. Preheat the oven to 425°F.

6 Brush the rolls with milk and sprinkle sea salt over the top. Bake in the preheated oven for 15–20 minutes, or until firm and golden brown. Transfer the rolls to a wire rack to cool.

garlic & sage bread

ingredients

makes 1 loaf

1¾ cups whole-wheat bread flour,
    plus extra for dusting
1 envelope active dry yeast
3 tablespoons chopped fresh sage,
    plus extra whole leaves
    to garnish
2 teaspoons sea salt
3 garlic cloves, finely chopped
1 teaspoon honey
⅔ cup lukewarm water
vegetable oil, for brushing
cream cheese, to serve

method

1 Sift the flour into a bowl and tip in the bran from
   the sifter. Stir in the yeast, sage, and half the sea salt.
   Reserve 1 teaspoon of the garlic and stir the remainder
   into the bowl. Make a well in the center and pour in the
   honey and water. Stir until the dough begins to come
   together, then knead until it leaves the side of the bowl.
   Invert onto a lightly floured surface and knead well for
   about 10 minutes, or until smooth and elastic.

2 Brush a bowl with oil. Shape the dough into a ball,
   put it in the bowl, and cover. Let rise in a warm place
   for 1 hour, or until doubled in size.

3 Brush a baking sheet with oil. Invert the dough onto a
   lightly floured surface and knead for 2 minutes. Roll the
   dough into a long log shape, form into a ring, and put
   it onto the prepared baking sheet. Brush the outside of
   a bowl with oil and put it into the center of the ring to
   prevent it from closing up while the dough is rising.
   Cover with a dish towel and let rise in a warm place for
   30 minutes.

4 Preheat the oven to 400°F. Remove the bowl from
   the center of the loaf. Sprinkle the loaf with the
   remaining sea salt and the reserved garlic and bake
   for 25–30 minutes, or until firm and golden brown.
   Transfer to a wire rack to cool. Serve with cream cheese.

peanut butter bread with scallions & thyme

ingredients

makes 1 loaf

3²/₃ cups white bread flour, plus extra for dusting
1 envelope active dry yeast
1 teaspoon salt
1¼ cups lukewarm water
1 tablespoon olive oil
¼ cup chunky peanut butter
1 teaspoon dried thyme
3 scallions, finely chopped
vegetable oil, for brushing
butter, to serve

method

1 Sift the flour into a bowl and stir in the yeast and salt. Make a well in the center and stir in the water, oil, peanut butter, thyme, and scallions, mixing to a soft dough.

2 Invert the dough onto a lightly floured surface and knead well for about 10 minutes, or until smooth and elastic. Cover and let rest for 5 minutes.

3 Brush a baking sheet with oil. Shape the dough into an oval and place on the prepared baking sheet. Slash the top of the dough at intervals with a sharp knife. Cover and let rest in a warm place for about 1 hour, or until doubled in size. Meanwhile, preheat the oven to 425°F.

4 Bake the loaf in the preheated oven for 15 minutes, then reduce the oven temperature to 400°F and bake for an additional 15–20 minutes, or until firm and golden brown. Transfer to a wire rack to cool. Serve with butter.

oat & potato bread

ingredients

makes 1 loaf

2 russet potatoes, cut into chunks
3¼ cups white bread flour,
    plus extra for dusting
1 envelope active dry yeast
1½ teaspoons salt
1½ tablespoons packed dark
    brown sugar
3 tablespoons rolled oats
2 tablespoons instant nonfat
    dry milk
3 tablespoons slightly salted
    butter, diced
1 cup lukewarm water
vegetable oil, for brushing

topping
1 tablespoon water
1 tablespoon rolled oats

method

1 Put the potatoes in a large saucepan, add water to cover, and bring to a boil. Cook for 20–25 minutes, or until tender. Drain the potatoes, then mash until smooth. Let cool.

2 Sift the flour into a bowl and stir in the yeast, salt, sugar, oats, and instant dry milk. Rub in the butter with your fingertips until the mixture resembles bread crumbs. Mix in the mashed potatoes, then add the water and mix to a soft dough.

3 Invert the dough onto a lightly floured surface and knead for 5–10 minutes, or until smooth and elastic. Put the dough in an oiled bowl, cover, and let rise in a warm place for 1 hour, or until doubled in size.

4 Brush a 9-inch loaf pan with oil. Invert the dough onto a lightly floured surface and knead lightly. Shape into a loaf and transfer to the prepared pan. Cover and let rise in a warm place for 30 minutes. Meanwhile, preheat the oven to 425°F.

5 Brush the loaf with water and sprinkle over the oats. Bake in the preheated oven for 25–30 minutes, or until firm and golden brown. Transfer to a wire rack to cool slightly. Serve warm.

hero rolls with parsley

ingredients

makes 4

3²/₃ cups white bread flour,
    plus extra for dusting
1½ teaspoons salt
1 envelope active dry yeast
1½ cups lukewarm water
1 tablespoon olive oil
2 tablespoons finely chopped
    fresh parsley
vegetable oil, for brushing

method

1 Sift together the flour and salt into a bowl and stir in the yeast. Make a well in the center and add the water, olive oil, and parsley, mixing to a soft dough.

2 Invert the dough onto a lightly floured surface and knead for about 10 minutes, until smooth. Return the dough to the bowl, cover, and let rest for 5 minutes.

3 Brush a baking sheet with oil. Invert the dough and lightly knead, then divide into four pieces and shape each piece into a torpedo shape.

4 Place the rolls on the prepared baking sheet, allowing room for spreading. Cover and let rest in a warm place for about 1 hour, or until doubled in size. Meanwhile, preheat the oven to 425°F.

5 Bake the rolls in the preheated oven for 12–15 minutes, or until golden brown. Transfer to a wire rack to cool.

tapenade swirls

ingredients

makes 10

3⅔ cups white bread flour, plus extra for dusting
1½ teaspoons sea salt
1 envelope active dry yeast
1½ cups lukewarm water
2 tablespoons olive oil
⅓ cup store-bought green olive tapenade
½ teaspoon crushed red pepper
cornmeal, for sprinkling
2 tablespoons finely grated Parmesan cheese

method

1 Sift the flour into a bowl and stir in the salt and yeast. Make a well in the center and add the water and oil, mixing to a soft dough.

2 Invert the dough onto a lightly floured surface and knead for about 10 minutes, or until smooth. Return the dough to the bowl, cover, and let rest for 5 minutes.

3 Invert the dough onto a lightly floured surface and roll out to a 14 x 18-inch rectangle. Spread the tapenade evenly over the dough to within ½ inch of the edges. Sprinkle with the crushed red pepper.

4 Roll up the dough from one long side to enclose the filling, like a jelly roll. Sprinkle a large baking sheet with cornmeal.

5 Using a sharp knife, cut the dough into ten thick slices and arrange, cut-side down, on the prepared baking sheet. Cover and let rest in a warm place for about 1 hour, or until doubled in size. Meanwhile, preheat the oven to 425°F.

6 Sprinkle the slices with the cheese, then bake in the preheated oven for 20–25 minutes, or until well risen and golden brown. Transfer to a wire rack to cool.

olive bread

ingredients

makes 2 medium loaves

6½ cups white bread flour,
   plus extra for dusting
1 teaspoon salt
1 envelope active dry yeast
3 teaspoons sesame seeds
½ teaspoon dried oregano
3 tablespoons olive oil, plus extra
   for brushing
2½ cups lukewarm water
2¼ cups coarsely chopped,
   pitted Greek olives

method

1 Sift together the flour and salt into a large bowl, and stir in the yeast, 2 teaspoons of the sesame seeds, and the oregano. Add the olive oil and gradually add the water to form a firm dough.

2 Invert the dough onto a lightly floured work surface and knead for 10 minutes, or until smooth. Put the dough in a clean bowl, cover, and let rise in a warm place for about 1 hour, or until doubled in size.

3 Brush a baking sheet with oil. Invert the dough onto a lightly floured work surface and knead gently to knock out the air, then knead in the olives. Divide the dough into two and shape each half into a smooth circle. Place on the prepared baking sheet, cover, and let rest in a warm place for about 30 minutes, or until doubled in size. Meanwhile, preheat the oven to 425°F.

4 Using a sharp knife, make slashes across the top of each loaf, then lightly brush with olive oil and sprinkle the remaining sesame seeds on top.

5 Bake in the preheated oven for 10 minutes, then reduce the temperature to 375°F and bake for an additional 25 minutes, or until firm and golden brown. Transfer to wire racks to cool.

pesto & olive soda bread

ingredients

makes 1 loaf

2³/₄ cups all-purpose flour
2 cups whole-wheat flour
1 teaspoon baking soda
¹/₂ teaspoon salt
3 tablespoons pesto
1¹/₄ cups buttermilk
1 cup coarsely chopped,
   pitted green olives
olive oil, for brushing
milk, for glazing

method

1 Preheat the oven to 400°F. Brush a baking sheet with oil. Sift together the flours, baking soda, and salt into a bowl, adding back any bran from the sifter.

2 Combine the pesto and buttermilk. Stir into the flour with the olives, mixing to a soft dough. Add more liquid, if needed.

3 Shape the dough into an 8-inch circle and place on the prepared baking sheet. Flatten slightly and cut a deep cross in the top with a sharp knife.

4 Brush with milk and bake in the preheated oven for 30–35 minutes, or until firm and golden brown.

variation

Replace the pesto and olives with 2 tablespoons of freshly chopped dill leaves and 2 tablespoons of poppy seeds. Add to the dry ingredients in step 1, reserving a teaspoon of poppy seeds to sprinkle over the top of the loaf in step 3.

olive oil bread with cheese

ingredients

makes 1 loaf

2 envelopes dried yeast
1 teaspoon sugar
1 cup lukewarm water
2½ cups white bread flour
1 teaspoon salt
3 tablespoons olive oil, plus extra
　　for brushing
8 ounces pecorino cheese, cubed
½ tablespoon fennel seeds,
　　lightly crushed

method

1 Mix the yeast with the sugar and ½ cup of the water. Set aside for about 15 minutes.

2 Sift together the flour with the salt into a bowl. Make a well in the center. Add 1 tablespoon of the oil, the yeast mixture, and the remaining water and mix together to form a smooth dough. Knead the dough for 4 minutes.

3 Brush a baking sheet with oil. Divide the dough into two equal portions. Roll out each portion to form a circle ¼ inch thick. Place one circle on the prepared baking sheet.

4 Sprinkle the cheese and half of the fennel seeds evenly over the circle. Place the second circle of dough on top and squeeze the edges together to seal, so that the filling does not leak during the cooking time.

5 Using a sharp knife, make a few slashes in the top of the dough and brush with the remaining oil.

6 Sprinkle with the remaining fennel seeds and set aside to rise for 20–30 minutes. Meanwhile, preheat the oven to 400°F.

7 Bake in the preheated oven for 30 minutes, or until golden brown. Serve immediately.

cheese corn bread

ingredients

makes 1 loaf

¾ cup all-purpose flour
1 tablespoon baking powder
pinch of salt
¾ cup cornmeal
1 cup shredded cheddar cheese or
   Monterey Jack cheese
2 eggs, beaten
1¼ cups milk
4 tablespoons butter, melted,
   plus extra for greasing

method

1 Preheat the oven to 400°F. Grease a 9-inch loaf pan with butter and line the bottom with wax paper.

2 Sift together the flour, baking powder, and salt into a bowl and stir in the cornmeal and cheese. Make a well in the center. Add the eggs, milk, and butter to the well. Gradually incorporate the dry ingredients into the liquid until smooth.

3 Pour the batter into the prepared pan and bake in the preheated oven for 40–45 minutes, or until firm and golden brown.

4 Let cool in the pan for 10 minutes before inverting onto a wire rack to cool completely.

scallion & parmesan corn bread

ingredients

makes 1 loaf

oil, for brushing
1 cup cornmeal
1 cup all-purpose flour
4 teaspoons baking powder
2 teaspoons celery salt
²/₃ cup freshly grated
    Parmesan cheese
2 eggs, beaten
1³/₄ cups milk
4 tablespoons butter, melted
1 bunch scallions, chopped
pepper

method

1 Preheat the oven to 375°F. Brush a 9-inch square baking pan with oil. Sift the cornmeal, flour, baking powder, celery salt, and pepper into a bowl and stir in ½ cup of the Parmesan cheese. Beat together the eggs, milk, and melted butter. Add the egg mixture to the dry ingredients and stir well to mix evenly.

2 Stir in the chopped scallions and spread the batter evenly into the baking pan. Sprinkle the remaining Parmesan over the batter. Bake in the preheated oven for 30–35 minutes, or until firm and golden.

cheese, herb & scallion rolls

ingredients

makes 10–12

1⅔ cups white bread flour, plus extra if needed

1¾ cups multigrain or malted wheat flour

1½ teaspoons salt

1 teaspoon dry mustard

1 envelope active dry yeast

2 tablespoons chopped fresh mixed herbs, such as oregano, thyme, and/or parsley

2 tablespoons finely chopped scallions

1–1½ cups shredded cheddar or Monterey Jack cheese

1¼ cups lukewarm water

oil, for brushing

pepper

method

1 Put the flours, salt, and mustard into a bowl and season with pepper. Stir in the yeast, herbs, scallions, and most of the cheese. Add the water to the dry ingredients and mix to form a firm dough, adding more flour, if necessary.

2 Knead until smooth and elastic. Cover and let rest in a warm place to rise for 1 hour, or until doubled in size.

3 Brush two baking sheets with oil. Meanwhile, preheat the oven to 400°F. Knead the dough until smooth. Divide into 10–12 pieces and shape into circular or long rolls, coils, or knots. Place on the prepared baking sheets, cover, and let rise until doubled in size.

4 Sprinkle with the rest of the cheese. Bake in the preheated oven for 15–20 minutes, or until golden brown. Transfer to a wire rack to cool.

irish potato bread

ingredients

makes 4 small loaves

7 russet potatoes
   (about 1¾ pounds)
2 tablespoons lightly salted butter
⅔ cup milk
½ teaspoon black pepper
1½ teaspoons dill seeds or caraway
   seeds (optional)
3¼ cups all-purpose flour,
   plus extra for dusting
5 teaspoons baking powder
salt

method

1 Preheat the oven to 375°F. Peel four of the potatoes, cut them into even chunks, and bring to a boil in a large saucepan of salted water. Cover and simmer gently for about 20 minutes, or until tender. Drain well and put back in the pan. Cover with a clean dish towel for a few minutes to get rid of excess moisture. Mash with the butter until smooth.

2 Meanwhile, peel the remaining three potatoes and shred. Wrap in a clean piece of cheesecloth and squeeze tightly to remove the moisture. Put the shredded potatoes in a large bowl with the milk, ¾ teaspoon of salt, the pepper, and dill seeds, if using. Beat in the mashed potatoes.

3 Sift the flour, baking powder, and 1½ teaspoons salt into the potato mixture. Mix to a smooth dough, adding a little more flour if the mixture is too soft.

4 Knead lightly, then shape into four flat, round loaves about 4 inches in diameter. Place on a nonstick baking sheet. Mark each loaf with a large cross. Bake in the preheated oven for 40 minutes, or until well risen and golden brown. Transfer to a wire rack to cool.

cheese & chive biscuits

ingredients

makes 12–14

vegetable oil, for brushing
4 cups all-purpose flour
1½ tablespoons baking powder
½ teaspoon salt
½ teaspoon pepper
1 stick butter, diced
1⅓ cups shredded sharp
    cheddar cheese
2 tablespoons snipped chives
1 extra-large egg
1 cup buttermilk or sour milk

method

1 Preheat the oven to 425°F. Brush a baking sheet with oil.

2 Sift together the flour, baking powder, salt, and pepper into a bowl. Add the butter and rub into the flour with your fingertips until it resembles fine bread crumbs. Stir in the cheese and chives.

3 Put the egg and buttermilk into a small bowl and beat together, then stir just enough into the dry ingredients to bind to a soft dough, lightly mixing.

4 Invert the dough and press together lightly until smooth. Form into a circle about 1 inch thick. Stamp out circles with a 2½-inch cutter and arrange on the prepared baking sheet.

5 Brush with the remaining buttermilk and egg mixture. Bake in the preheated oven for 12–15 minutes, or until firm and golden brown. Transfer to a wire rack to cool.

cheese & potato braid

ingredients

makes 1 loaf

1 russet potato, diced
2 envelopes active dry yeast
5 cups white bread flour,
    plus extra for dusting
1 tablespoon salt
2 cups vegetable stock
2 garlic cloves, crushed
2 tablespoons chopped
    fresh rosemary
1 cup shredded Swiss cheese
1 tablespoon vegetable oil,
    plus extra for brushing

method

1 Cook the potato in a saucepan of boiling water for 10 minutes, or until soft. Drain and mash the potato.

2 Transfer the mashed potato to a large mixing bowl. Stir the yeast, flour, salt, and stock into the mashed potato and mix together to form a smooth dough. Add the garlic, rosemary, and ⅔ cup of the cheese and knead the dough for 5 minutes. Make a hollow in the dough, pour in the oil, and knead the dough.

3 Cover the dough and let rise in a warm place for 1½ hours, or until doubled in size.

4 Brush a baking sheet with oil and lightly dust with flour. Knead the dough again and divide it into three equal portions. Roll each portion into a 14-inch log shape.

5 Press together one end of each of the log shapes, then braid the dough and fold the remaining ends underneath. Place the braid on the baking sheet, cover, and let rise for 30 minutes. Meanwhile, preheat the oven to 375°F.

6 Sprinkle the remaining cheese over the top of the braid and bake in the preheated oven for 40 minutes, or until firm and golden brown. Transfer to a wire rack to cool slightly and serve warm.

cheese & ham loaf

ingredients

makes 1 loaf

1¾ cups all-purpose flour
1 teaspoon salt
3¾ teaspoons baking powder
1 teaspoon paprika
6 tablespoons butter, diced,
    plus extra for greasing
1 cup shredded sharp
    cheddar cheese or Monterey
    Jack cheese, plus extra
    for serving
3 ounces smoked ham, chopped
2 eggs, beaten
⅔ cup milk

method

1 Preheat the oven to 350°F. Grease an 8½-inch loaf pan with a little butter and line the bottom with parchment paper.

2 Sift the flour, salt, baking powder, and paprika into a large mixing bowl.

3 Add the butter and rub it in with your fingertips until the mixture resembles fine bread crumbs. Stir in the cheese and ham.

4 Add the beaten eggs and milk to the dry ingredients in the bowl and mix well. Spoon the cheese and ham mixture into the prepared loaf pan.

5 Bake in the preheated oven for about 1 hour, or until the loaf is well risen and golden brown.

6 Let the bread cool in the pan, then invert and transfer to a wire rack to cool completely. Cut the bread into thick slices and serve with cheese.

variation

For a vegetarian option, replace the ham with 1 Pippin apple, peeled, cored, and cut into small chunks.

breads from around the world

irish stout bread

ingredients

makes 1 loaf

vegetable oil, for brushing
1¼ cups stout
1¾ cups white bread flour,
    plus extra for dusting
2 cups malted barley flour
1 envelope active dry yeast
1½ teaspoons salt

method

1 Brush a 9-inch loaf pan with oil. Pour the stout into a saucepan and heat until lukewarm (it should feel neither hot nor cold to the touch). Remove from the heat.

2 Sift the white flour and barley flour into a bowl and stir in the yeast and salt. Make a well in the center and add the stout, mixing to a soft dough.

3 Invert the dough onto a lightly floured surface and knead for about 10 minutes, until smooth, then return to the bowl, cover, and let rest for 5 minutes.

4 Invert the dough onto a lightly floured surface and lightly knead, then shape into an oval and place in the prepared pan. Cover and let rest in a warm place for about 1 hour, or until doubled in size. Meanwhile, preheat the oven to 450°F.

5 Place the loaf in the preheated oven, then spray the oven with water. Bake for 10 minutes, then reduce the oven temperature to 400°F and bake for an additional 20–25 minutes, or until golden brown. Transfer to a wire rack to cool.

irish soda bread

ingredients

makes 1 loaf

butter, for greasing
3²/₃ cups all-purpose flour,
    plus extra for dusting
1 teaspoon salt
1 teaspoon baking soda
1¾ cups buttermilk

method

1 Preheat the oven to 425°F and lightly grease a baking sheet.

2 Sift together the flour, salt, and baking soda into a bowl. Make a well in the center of the dry ingredients and pour in most of the buttermilk.

3 Mix well together using your hands. The dough should be soft but not too wet. If necessary, add the remaining buttermilk.

4 Invert the dough onto a lightly floured surface and knead it lightly. Shape into an 8-inch circle.

5 Place the bread on the prepared baking sheet, cut a cross in the top, and bake in the preheated oven for 25–30 minutes, until firm and golden brown. Transfer to a wire rack to cool.

variation

To make a fruit soda bread, add 1 tablespoon of sugar, the zest of an orange, and ¾ cup raisins to the dry ingredients in step 2.

welsh bara brith

ingredients

makes 1 loaf

butter, for greasing
¾ cup milk
4 teaspoons dried yeast
½ cup firmly packed brown sugar
3¼ cups white bread flour
½ teaspoon salt
1 stick butter, diced
1½ cups mixed dried fruit, such as
    golden raisins, dried currants,
    and raisins
⅓ cup candied peel
1 teaspoon ground allspice
1 egg, beaten

method

1 Grease a 9-inch loaf pan. Warm the milk in a saucepan until lukewarm and add the yeast with 1 teaspoon of the sugar. Mix well and let rest in a warm place for 15 minutes, or until frothy.

2 Sift the flour and salt into a bowl. Rub the butter into the flour mixture until it resembles bread crumbs, then add the remaining sugar, dried fruit, candied peel, and allspice and stir well. Add the beaten egg and the frothy yeast mixture and mix to form a soft dough.

3 Turn the dough out onto a floured surface and knead until smooth. Replace the dough in the bowl, cover, and let rest in a warm place for 1–1½ hours, or until doubled in size. Meanwhile, preheat the oven to 375°F.

4 Turn the dough out again and knead lightly. Shape the dough into a rectangle the length of the pan and three times the width. Fold the dough into three lengthwise and put it in the pan with the seam underneath. Cover and let rise in a warm place for 30–40 minutes.

5 Bake toward the bottom of the oven for 30 minutes. Turn the loaf around and cover the top with aluminum foil if it is getting too brown. Continue to cook for an additional 30–40 minutes. Transfer to a wire rack to cool.

french baguettes

ingredients

makes 2 loaves

3¼ cups white bread flour,
   plus extra for dusting
1½ teaspoons salt
1 envelope active dry yeast
1⅓ cups lukewarm water
vegetable oil, for brushing

method

1 Sift the flour and salt into a bowl and stir in the yeast. Make a well in the center and pour in the water. Stir well until the dough begins to come together, then knead with your hands until it leaves the side of the bowl. Invert onto a lightly floured surface and knead well for about 10 minutes, or until smooth and elastic.

2 Brush a bowl with oil. Put the dough in the bowl, cover, and let rest in a warm place for 1 hour, or until doubled in size. Invert onto a lightly floured surface and knead for 1–2 minutes. Cut the dough in half, shape each piece into a ball, and roll out into a rectangle. From one long side of a dough rectangle, fold one-third over, then fold over the other side. Press gently. Fold the other rectangle in the same way. Cover and let rest for 10 minutes. Repeat the rolling and folding twice again, letting the dough rest for 10 minutes each time. Gently roll and stretch each piece of dough until it is about 12 inches long and an even thickness. Cover and let rise for 30–40 minutes.

3 Meanwhile, preheat the oven to 450°F. Brush one or two baking sheets with oil. Carefully roll the loaves onto the baking sheets and slash the tops with a sharp knife. Spray the oven with water and bake for 15–20 minutes, or until golden brown. Transfer to a wire rack to cool.

brioche braid

ingredients

makes 1 loaf

2½ cups white bread flour,
    plus extra for dusting
½ teaspoon salt
2 tablespoons sugar
1 envelope active dry yeast
1 stick unsalted butter, chilled and
    diced, plus extra for greasing
2 eggs, beaten
⅓ cup warm milk
olive oil, for brushing
beaten egg, for glazing

method

1 Sift the flour and salt into a large bowl. Stir in the sugar and dried yeast. Add the butter and rub into the flour with your fingertips until it resembles bread crumbs. Make a well in the center and pour the eggs and milk into the bowl.

2 Stir well to make a soft dough. Turn the dough onto a lightly floured surface and knead for 5–10 minutes, until smooth and elastic, sprinkling with a little more flour if the dough becomes sticky.

3 Brush a large baking sheet with oil. Divide the dough into three equal pieces and shape each into a rope about 14 inches long. Place the ropes side by side and press them together at one end. Braid the ropes, then pinch the ends together.

4 Transfer the braid to the baking sheet, cover loosely with oiled plastic wrap, and let rest in a warm place for about 1 hour, or until doubled in size.

5 Preheat the oven to 375°F. Brush the braid with the beaten egg. Bake in the preheated oven for 30–35 minutes, or until risen and golden brown, covering loosely with aluminum foil after 25 minutes to prevent it from overbrowning. Serve warm.

salted pretzels

ingredients

makes 16

vegetable oil, for brushing
3²/₃ cups white bread flour,
    plus extra for dusting
1 envelope active dry yeast
1½ teaspoons salt
1 tablespoon packed dark
    brown sugar
1 tablespoon olive oil
1½ cups lukewarm water, plus
    1 tablespoon for brushing
1 teaspoon baking soda
1 egg
coarse sea salt, for sprinkling

method

1 Brush two large baking sheets with oil. Sift the flour into a bowl and stir in the yeast, salt, and sugar. Make a well in the center and stir in the oil with just enough water to mix to a soft dough.

2 Invert the dough onto a lightly floured surface and knead for about 10 minutes, until smooth. Return to the bowl, then cover and let rest for 5 minutes.

3 Divide the dough into 16 pieces and roll each piece into a 15-inch rope. Lift both ends of the rope and twist together, then drop the ends back over the loop to make pretzel shapes.

4 Place the pretzels on the prepared baking sheets, allowing room for spreading, then cover and let rest in a warm place for 20 minutes. Meanwhile, preheat the oven to 425°F.

5 Bring a large saucepan of water to a boil, add the baking soda, then add the pretzels and cook for about 20 seconds each, turning once. Remove and drain well, then return to the baking sheets.

6 Beat the egg with the 1 tablespoon of water and brush over the pretzels, then sprinkle with salt. Bake in the preheated oven for 15–20 minutes, or until golden brown. Transfer to a wire rack to cool.

challah

ingredients

makes 1 loaf

vegetable oil, for brushing
3²/₃ cups white bread flour,
    plus extra for dusting
1 teaspoon ground cinnamon
1 envelope active dry yeast
1 teaspoon salt
1 cup lukewarm water
¹/₃ cup honey
1 egg, beaten
2 tablespoons olive oil

to glaze

1 egg yolk
pinch of salt
1 tablespoon water

method

1 Brush a large baking sheet with oil. Sift the flour into a bowl and stir in the cinnamon, yeast, and salt. Make a well in the center and add the water, honey, egg, and oil, mixing to a soft dough.

2 Invert the dough onto a lightly floured surface and knead for about 10 minutes, or until smooth. Return to the bowl, then cover and let rest in a warm place for 1 hour, or until doubled in size.

3 Invert the dough onto a lightly floured surface and lightly knead, then divide into six pieces and shape each piece into a 14-inch-long roll. Pinch together the ends of the dough, then braid together, overlapping from alternate sides. Tuck the end underneath and place on the prepared baking sheet.

4 Cover and let rest in a warm place for about 1 hour, or until doubled in size. Meanwhile, preheat the oven to 425°F.

5 Bake in the preheated oven for 15 minutes, then reduce the oven temperature to 375°F. To glaze, beat the egg yolk with the salt and water, brush over the loaf, then return to the oven and bake for an additional 15–20 minutes, or until firm and a rich golden brown. Transfer to a wire rack to cool.

kulich

ingredients

makes 2 loaves

oil, for brushing
3²/₃ cups white bread flour,
    plus extra for dusting
1 envelope active dry yeast
1¼ cups lukewarm milk
1 teaspoon salt
½ cup sugar
6 tablespoons butter, melted
    and cooled
2 egg yolks
½ cup golden raisins
½ cup slivered almonds
grated rind of 2 oranges
grated rind and juice of 1 lemon
confectioners' sugar and chopped
    candied fruit, to decorate

method

1 Brush two clean terra-cotta flowerpots with a top diameter of 6 inches with oil and line with nonstick parchment paper. Place half the flour in a bowl with the yeast and stir in the milk to make a smooth batter. Cover and let rest in a warm place for about 20 minutes, or until frothy.

2 Add the remaining flour, salt, sugar, butter, egg yolks, golden raisins, almonds, orange rind, lemon rind, and 2 tablespoons of the lemon juice and mix to a soft dough. Invert onto a lightly floured surface and knead for about 10 minutes, or until smooth.

3 Divide the dough into two pieces and shape to fit the flowerpots. Cover and let rest in a warm place for about 1½ hours, or until risen to the top of the flowerpots. Meanwhile, preheat the oven to 425°F.

4 Bake in the preheated oven for 10 minutes, then reduce the oven temperature to 350°F and bake for an additional 25–30 minutes, or until firm and golden brown. Invert and transfer to a wire rack to cool.

5 Mix 2 teaspoons of the lemon juice with enough confectioners' sugar to make a smooth icing, then spoon it over the kulich and sprinkle with the candied fruit.

tuscan unsalted bread

ingredients

makes 1 large or
2 smaller loaves

3²/₃ cups white bread flour,
     plus extra for dusting
1 envelope active dry yeast
2 tablespoons olive oil, plus extra
     for brushing
1¹/₄ cups lukewarm water

method

1 Mix together the flour and yeast in a bowl. Make a
well in the center. Mix together the olive oil and water
in a small bowl and pour into the well. Gradually
mix the liquid into the flour mixture with a spatula.
Gather together the mixture with your hands to
form a soft dough.

2 Invert the dough onto a lightly floured work surface
and knead for 5–7 minutes, or until smooth and
elastic. Return the dough to the bowl and cover, then
let rise in a warm place for 1 hour, or until doubled
in size. Invert and gently knead again for 1 minute,
or until smooth.

3 Preheat the oven to 400°F. Brush one or two baking
sheets with oil. Shape the dough into one large oval
or two smaller ovals and transfer to the prepared
sheet or sheets. Cover and let rise in a warm place for
30 minutes.

4 Make several slashes in the top of the bread with
a sharp knife. Bake in the preheated oven for
30–35 minutes (or 20–25 minutes for two loaves).
If the bread is getting too brown, reduce the
temperature a little. Transfer to a wire rack to cool.

ciabatta

ingredients

makes 3 loaves

1¾ cups lukewarm water
¼ cup lukewarm low-fat milk
3⅔ cups white bread flour
1 envelope active dry yeast
2 teaspoons salt
3 tablespoons olive oil

biga

2½ cups white bread flour,
    plus extra for dusting
1¼ teaspoons active dry yeast
1 cup lukewarm water

method

1 First, make the biga. Sift the flour into a bowl, stir in the yeast, and make a well in the center. Pour in the water and stir until the dough comes together. Invert onto a lightly floured surface and knead for 5 minutes, or until smooth and elastic. Put the dough into a bowl, cover, and let rise in a warm place for 12 hours.

2 Using a wooden spoon, gradually mix the water and milk into the biga. Gradually mix in the flour and yeast with your hand, adding them a little at a time. Finally, mix in the salt and oil. The dough will be wet, but do not add extra flour. Cover and let rise in a warm place for 2 hours, or until doubled in size.

3 Dust three baking sheets with flour. Using a spatula, divide the dough among the prepared baking sheets without knocking out the air. With lightly floured hands, gently pull and shape each piece of dough into a rectangular loaf, then flatten slightly. Dust the tops of the loaves with flour and let rise in a warm place for 30 minutes. Meanwhile, preheat the oven to 425°F.

4 Bake in the preheated oven for 25–30 minutes, or until the crust is lightly golden. Transfer to wire racks to cool.

mini focaccia

ingredients

makes 4 loaves

2½ cups white bread flour,
  plus extra for dusting
1 envelope active dry yeast
½ teaspoon salt
1 cup lukewarm water
3 tablespoons olive oil, plus extra
  for brushing
1 cup halved, pitted ripe green
  or black olives

topping

2 red onions, sliced
2 tablespoons olive oil
1 teaspoon sea salt
1 tablespoon fresh thyme leaves

method

1 Sift the flour into a bowl and stir in the yeast and salt. Make a well in the center and gradually stir in the water and 2 tablespoons of the olive oil to make a dough. Invert the dough onto a floured work surface and knead for 5 minutes.

2 Wash the bowl and lightly brush with olive oil. Place the dough in the oiled bowl, cover, and let rest in a warm place for 1–1½ hours, or until doubled in size.

3 Brush a baking sheet with oil. Invert the dough onto a lightly floured surface and knead for 1–2 minutes. Knead half of the olives into the dough, divide the dough into quarters, and shape the quarters into circles. Carefully transfer them to the prepared baking sheet. Using a lightly oiled finger, poke indentations all over the surface of the loaves.

4 To make the topping, sprinkle the red onions and remaining olives over the circles. Drizzle the remaining oil over the top and sprinkle with the sea salt and thyme leaves. Cover and let stand for 30 minutes. Meanwhile, preheat the oven to 375°F.

5 Bake in the preheated oven, for 20–25 minutes, or until golden brown. Transfer to a wire rack to cool.

margherita pizza

ingredients

makes 1 pizza

1⅓ cups all-purpose flour,
    plus extra for dusting
1 teaspoon salt
1 teaspoon active dry yeast
1 tablespoon olive oil, plus extra
    for brushing
⅓ cup lukewarm water

topping

¾ cup store-bought pizza sauce
1 garlic clove, thinly sliced
2 ounces mozzarella cheese,
    thinly sliced
1 teaspoon dried oregano
salt and pepper
fresh basil sprigs, to garnish

method

1 Sift together the flour and salt into a bowl and stir in the yeast. Make a well in the center and pour in the oil and water. Stir well until the dough begins to come together, then knead with your hands until it leaves the side of the bowl. Invert onto a lightly floured surface and knead well for 5–10 minutes, or until smooth and elastic.

2 Brush a bowl with oil. Shape the dough into a ball, put it in the bowl, cover, and let rise in a warm place for 1 hour, or until dough has doubled in size.

3 Brush a baking sheet with oil. Invert the dough onto a lightly floured surface and knead for 1 minute. Roll or press out the dough to a 10-inch circle. Place on the prepared baking sheet and push up the edge slightly all around. Cover and let rise in a warm place for 10 minutes. Meanwhile, preheat the oven to 400°F.

4 Spread the pizza sauce over the pizza crust almost to the edge. Sprinkle the garlic over the sauce, add the cheese, sprinkle with the oregano, and season with salt and pepper. Bake the pizza in the preheated oven for 15–20 minutes, or until the crust is crisp and golden brown. Brush the crust with oil, garnish with basil sprigs, and serve immediately.

calzone

ingredients

makes 4

3¼ cups white bread flour,
    plus extra for dusting
1 envelope active dry yeast
1 teaspoon salt
1¼ cups lukewarm water
1 tablespoon olive oil
vegetable oil, for brushing

filling

1 tablespoon olive oil
1 red onion, thinly sliced
1 garlic clove, crushed
4 plum tomatoes, chopped
2 tablespoons tomato paste
8 ounces cooked ham, diced
2 tablespoons chopped fresh
    basil leaves
8 ounces mozzarella cheese,
    chopped
salt and pepper

method

1 Sift the flour into a bowl and stir in the yeast and salt. Make a well in the center and add the water and oil, mixing to a soft dough.

2 Invert the dough onto a lightly floured surface and knead for about 10 minutes, until smooth. Return to the bowl, cover, and let rest in a warm place for 1 hour, or until doubled in size.

3 To make the filling, heat the oil in a skillet, add the onion and garlic, and gently sauté for 5 minutes. Add the tomatoes and simmer, stirring, for 5 minutes, or until any liquid has evaporated. Remove from the heat, add the tomato paste, ham, and basil, and season with salt and pepper.

4 Preheat the oven to 425°F and brush two baking sheets with oil. Invert the dough onto a lightly floured surface and lightly knead. Divide into four pieces and shape each piece into an 8-inch circle.

5 Spoon the filling onto one side of each circle and top with cheese. Brush the edges with water, fold over to enclose the filling, and pinch the edges together to seal. Place on the prepared baking sheets and pierce a hole in each calzone to let the steam escape. Bake in the preheated oven for 15–20 minutes, or until crisp and golden brown. Serve warm.

breadsticks with nigella seeds

ingredients

makes about 24

1½ cups white bread flour
1 cup whole-wheat bread flour
1 envelope active dry yeast
1½ teaspoons salt
3½ tablespoons nigella seeds or
    celery seeds
1 tablespoon packed dark
    brown sugar
1¼ cups lukewarm water
2 tablespoons olive oil, plus extra
    for brushing
coarse sea salt, for sprinkling

method

1 Line two large baking sheets with nonstick parchment paper.

2 Sift the white flour into a bowl, add the whole-wheat flour, and stir in the yeast, salt, nigella seeds, and sugar. Make a well in the center and add the water and oil, mixing to a soft dough.

3 Invert the dough onto a lightly oiled surface and lightly knead for about 5 minutes, or until just smooth. Return to the bowl, cover, and let stand for about 1 hour, or until doubled in size. Meanwhile, preheat the oven to 350°F.

4 Invert the dough onto a lightly oiled surface and lightly knead. Roll out to a ½-inch thick square. Cut into long, pencil-thin strips (a pizza wheel is useful here), then arrange down the length of the prepared baking sheets, lightly twisting.

5 Brush with oil and sprinkle with sea salt. Bake in the preheated oven for 25–30 minutes, or until golden brown and crisp. Carefully transfer to a wire rack to cool.

pita breads

ingredients

makes 6–8

2½ cups white bread flour,
    plus extra for dusting
1½ teaspoons salt
1 teaspoon sugar
1 teaspoon active dry yeast
1 tablespoon olive oil, plus extra
    for brushing
1 cup lukewarm water

method

1 Sift together the flour and salt into a bowl and stir in the sugar and yeast. Make a well in the center and pour in the oil and water. Stir well until the dough begins to come together, then knead with your hands until it leaves the side of the bowl. Invert onto a lightly floured surface and knead well for about 10 minutes, or until smooth and elastic.

2 Shape the dough into a ball, put into an oiled bowl, and cover. Let rise in a warm place for 1 hour, or until the dough has doubled in size.

3 Invert onto a lightly floured surface. Divide the dough into six to eight pieces and shape each piece into a ball. Cover and let rest for 10 minutes.

4 With floured hands, slightly flatten a dough ball and roll out on a lightly floured surface to an oval about 6 inches long and ¼ inch thick. Place on a lightly floured dish towel, sprinkle lightly with flour, and cover with another dish towel. Repeat with the remaining dough balls and let rise for 30 minutes.

5 Meanwhile, put two or three baking sheets in the oven and preheat to 450°F. Transfer the pita breads to the heated baking sheets, spacing them well apart, and bake for 5 minutes, or until puffed up and golden brown. Transfer to wire racks to cool.

sesame bread rings

ingredients

makes 16

vegetable oil, for brushing
3²/₃ cups white bread flour, plus
    extra for dusting
1 envelope active dry yeast
2 teaspoons salt
1 teaspoon ground cumin
1 teaspoon ground coriander
1½ cups lukewarm water
2 tablespoons olive oil
1 egg, beaten
½ cup sesame seeds

method

1 Brush two to three large baking sheets with oil. Sift the flour into a bowl and stir in the yeast, salt, cumin, and coriander. Make a well in the center and add the water and oil, mixing to a soft dough.

2 Invert the dough onto a lightly floured surface and knead for about 10 minutes, or until smooth. Return the dough to the bowl, then cover and let rest for 5 minutes.

3 Invert the dough, divide into 16 pieces, and shape each piece into a 14-inch rope. Shape into rings, pinching together the ends.

4 Beat the egg with 1 tablespoon of cold water and brush over the rings, then dip into the sesame seeds to coat and place on the prepared baking sheets. Cover and let rest in a warm place for about 1 hour, or until well risen and springy to the touch. Meanwhile, preheat the oven to 425°F.

5 Bake in the preheated oven for 10–15 minutes, or until firm and golden brown. Transfer to wire racks to cool.

naan

ingredients

makes 10

6¼ cups white bread flour
1 tablespoon baking powder
1 teaspoon sugar
1 teaspoon salt
1½ cups lukewarm water
1 egg
¼ cup melted ghee or vegetable
   oil, plus a little extra for oiling
   and brushing
fresh cilantro sprigs, to garnish

method

1 Sift the flour, baking powder, sugar, and salt into a bowl and make a well in the center. Mix together the water and egg, beating until the egg breaks up and is blended with the liquid.

2 Slowly add the liquid mixture to the well in the dry ingredients, using your fingers to draw in the flour from the sides, or until a stiff, heavy dough forms. Shape the dough into a ball, cover, and let rest for 30 minutes.

3 Invert the dough onto a surface brushed with melted ghee and flatten with a rolling pin. Gradually sprinkle the dough with the melted ghee and knead to work it in, little by little. Shape the dough into ten equal balls, cover, and let rise for 1 hour. Meanwhile, preheat the oven to 450°F or its highest setting.

4 Using a lightly greased rolling pin, roll the dough balls into teardrop shapes, about ⅛ inch thick. Brush two baking sheets with ghee and arrange the naans on the prepared sheets. Bake in the preheated oven for 5–6 minutes, until the naans are golden brown and lightly puffed. Serve immediately, garnished with fresh cilantro sprigs.

chile corn bread

ingredients

makes 1 loaf

1 cup cornmeal
½ cup all-purpose flour
1 tablespoon baking powder
1 small onion, finely chopped
1–2 fresh green chiles, such as
    jalapeño, seeded and chopped
¼ cup vegetable oil
¾ cup canned cream-style corn
1 cup sour cream
2 eggs, beaten

method

1 Preheat the oven to 350°F.

2 Place the cornmeal, flour, and baking powder in a large bowl, then stir in the onion and chiles.

3 Heat the oil in a heavy 9-inch skillet with a heatproof handle, tipping the skillet to coat the bottom and sides with the oil.

4 Make a well in the center of the ingredients in the bowl. Add the corn, sour cream, and eggs, then pour in the hot oil from the skillet. Stir lightly until combined. Pour the mixture into the hot skillet and smooth the surface with a spatula.

5 Bake in the preheated oven for 35–40 minutes, or until a toothpick inserted into the center comes out clean. Cut into wedges and serve warm from the skillet.

wheat tortillas

ingredients

makes 10

2 cups all-purpose flour,
    plus extra for dusting
½ teaspoon baking powder
½ teaspoon salt
4 tablespoons lard, vegetable
    shortening, or butter
¾ cup lukewarm water
vegetable oil, for brushing

method

1 Sift the flour, baking powder, and salt into a bowl and evenly rub in the lard with your fingertips. Make a well in the center and add enough water to mix to a soft, slightly sticky, dough.

2 Invert the dough onto a lightly floured surface and lightly knead until smooth, then wrap in oiled plastic wrap and let rest for 30 minutes.

3 Invert the dough and divide into ten pieces. Roll each piece into a thin 8-inch circle.

4 Heat a flat griddle pan or heavy skillet until hot. Lightly brush with oil, add a tortilla, and cook for a few seconds until bubbles appear on the surface, then turn and cook the other side until lightly browned.

5 Cook the remaining tortillas in the same way, keeping the cooked ones warm under a clean dish towel. Serve the tortillas warm.

dessert breads

pecan & cranberry stollen

ingredients

makes 1 loaf

3 cups white bread flour,
    plus extra for dusting
1/2 teaspoon salt
1/2 teaspoon allspice
4 tablespoons butter, diced
2 tablespoons sugar
1 envelope active dry yeast
1/3 cup dried cranberries
1/2 cup chopped pecans
1 egg, beaten
1 cup lukewarm milk
vegetable oil, for brushing
5 ounces marzipan (about 1/2 cup)
confectioners' sugar, for sprinkling

method

1 Sift the flour, salt, and allspice into a bowl and evenly rub in the butter. Stir in the sugar and yeast, then add the cranberries, nuts, egg, and enough milk to mix to a soft dough.

2 Invert the dough onto a lightly floured surface and knead for about 10 minutes, until smooth. Return to the bowl, cover, and let rise in a warm place for about 1 hour, or until doubled in size. Brush a large baking sheet with oil.

3 Invert the dough onto a lightly floured surface and lightly knead, then roll out to a 9 x 7-inch rectangle, about 1/2 inch thick. Roll the marzipan into a log shape about 8 inches long, then lay it down the middle of the dough rectangle and fold over the sides to enclose it.

4 Place the stollen, seam-side down, on the prepared baking sheet, cover, and let rest in a warm place for about 1 hour, or until well risen. Meanwhile, preheat the oven to 375°F.

5 Bake in the preheated oven for 30–35 minutes, or until golden brown and the bottom sounds hollow when tapped. Transfer to a wire rack to cool, then sprinkle with confectioners' sugar to serve.

banana walnut bread

ingredients

makes 1 loaf

butter, for greasing
1 cup walnut oil
½ cup raw brown sugar
2 eggs
3 very ripe bananas, mashed
2¼ cups all-purpose flour
1 teaspoon baking soda
1 teaspoon baking powder
½ teaspoon salt
3 tablespoons milk
2 tablespoons plain yogurt
½ teaspoon vanilla extract
½ cup walnuts, crushed

method

1 Preheat the oven to 350°F. Grease an 8½-inch loaf pan and line with parchment paper.

2 In a large bowl, cream together the oil and sugar until blended, then beat in the eggs and mashed bananas.

3 Combine the flour, baking soda, baking powder, and salt, then add to the banana mixture. Pour in the milk, yogurt, and vanilla extract and mix together until blended. Stir in the crushed walnuts, then pour the batter into the prepared pan.

4 Bake for 50 minutes to 1 hour, or until a toothpick inserted into the middle comes out clean. Cool for 10 minutes in the pan, then invert the bread and finish cooling on a wire rack.

apple & hazelnut bread

ingredients

makes 1 loaf

butter, for greasing
1½ cups lukewarm water
1 teaspoon sugar
1 envelope active dry yeast
3¼ cups all-purpose white flour,
    plus extra for dusting
3¼ cups whole-wheat flour
5 teaspoons baking powder
½ teaspoon sea salt
1 cup toasted hazelnuts, chopped
½ cup chopped dried apple
1 Pippin apple, grated

method

1 Grease an 8½-inch loaf pan and line with parchment paper. Put ½ cup of the lukewarm water in a small bowl, stir in the sugar and yeast, and let rest for 15 minutes.

2 Mix together the flours, baking powder, salt, nuts, dried apple, and fresh apple in a large bowl. Make a well in the center, pour in the yeast mixture, and gradually work into the flour mixture. Mix in the remaining water and bring together to form a soft dough.

3 Invert onto a floured work surface and knead briefly. Shape the dough into a rectangle and place in the prepared pan. Cover with a warm, damp cloth and set aside in a warm place for 40 minutes, until the dough has risen. Meanwhile, preheat the oven to 400°F.

4 Remove the cloth and bake the loaf in the preheated oven for 40 minutes. Carefully lift out of the pan and return the loaf to the oven, upside down, for 10–15 minutes—the loaf should sound hollow when tapped on the bottom. Remove from the oven and let cool on a wire rack.

citrus bread

ingredients

makes 1 loaf

3¼ cups white bread flour, plus
    extra for dusting
½ teaspoon salt
¼ cup sugar
1 envelope active dry yeast
3½ tablespoons butter, diced,
    plus extra for greasing
⅓ cup orange juice
¼ cup lemon juice
¼ cup lime juice
⅓ cup lukewarm water
1 orange
1 lemon
1 lime
2 tablespoons honey, for glazing

method

1 Sift together the flour and salt into a large mixing bowl. Stir in the sugar and yeast.

2 Rub the butter into the mixture with your fingertips until the mixture resembles bread crumbs. Add the orange juice, lemon juice, lime juice, and water and bring together with your fingers to form a dough.

3 Invert the dough onto a lightly floured surface and knead for 5 minutes. Place the dough in a greased bowl, cover, and let rise in a warm place for about 1 hour, or until doubled in size. Lightly grease a baking sheet with butter.

4 Meanwhile, finely grate the rind of the orange, lemon, and lime. Knead the fruit rinds into the dough. Divide the dough into two balls, making one slightly bigger than the other. Place the larger ball on the prepared baking sheet and set the smaller one on top.

5 Push a floured finger through the center of the dough. Cover and let rise for about 40 minutes, or until springy to the touch. Meanwhile, preheat the oven to 425°F.

6 Bake in the preheated oven for 35 minutes. Remove from the oven and transfer to a wire rack to cool. Glaze with the honey.

pear & lemon braid

ingredients

makes 1 loaf

vegetable oil, for brushing
3²/₃ cups white bread flour,
    plus extra for dusting
1 teaspoon salt
2 tablespoons sugar
1 envelope active dry yeast
1½ cups lukewarm water
2 tablespoons butter, melted
finely grated rind of 2 lemons
½ cup chopped dried pears
milk, for glazing

method

1 Brush a large baking sheet with oil. Sift the flour into a bowl, add the salt and sugar, and stir in the yeast. Make a well in the center, add the water, butter, lemon rind, and pears and mix to a soft dough.

2 Invert the dough onto a lightly floured surface and knead for about 10 minutes, or until smooth. Return to the bowl, cover, and let rest for 5 minutes.

3 Invert the dough onto a lightly floured surface and lightly knead, then divide into three pieces. Roll each piece into a 20-inch rope. Braid the ropes loosely, pinching together the ends to hold in place.

4 Lift the braid onto the prepared baking sheet, cover, and let rest in a warm place for about 1 hour, or until doubled in size. Meanwhile, preheat the oven to 375°F.

5 Brush the braid with milk and bake in the preheated oven for 30–35 minutes, or until golden brown and firm. Transfer to a wire rack to cool.

oat & apricot breakfast rolls

ingredients

makes 8

vegetable oil, for brushing
2 cups white bread flour,
    plus extra for dusting
1 cup whole-wheat bread flour
1 cup rolled oats, plus extra
    for sprinkling
1 teaspoon salt
1 envelope active dry yeast
²⁄₃ cup lukewarm milk,
    plus extra for glazing
²⁄₃ cup lukewarm water
1 tablespoon honey
1 cup chopped dried apricots

method

1 Brush a baking sheet with oil. Sift the white flour into a large bowl, add the whole-wheat flour, oats, and salt, then stir in the yeast and make a well in the center. Pour the lukewarm milk and water into a small bowl, add the honey, and stir, then add to the dry ingredients with the apricots, mixing to a soft dough.

2 Invert the dough onto a lightly floured surface and knead for about 10 minutes, until smooth, then return to the bowl, cover, and let rest for 5 minutes.

3 Invert the dough and divide into eight pieces, then shape each piece into a ball and arrange on the prepared baking sheet. Cut a cross into the top of each roll with a sharp knife.

4 Cover and let rest in a warm place for about 1 hour, or until doubled in size. Meanwhile, preheat the oven to 425°F.

5 Brush the tops of the rolls with cold milk and sprinkle with oats. Bake the rolls in the preheated oven for 15–20 minutes, or until golden brown. Transfer to a wire rack to cool.

tropical fruit bread

ingredients

makes 1 loaf

2¾ cups white bread flour, plus extra for dusting
½ teaspoon salt
½ teaspoon ground ginger
½ cup wheat bran
1 envelope active dry yeast
2 tablespoons packed light brown sugar
2 tablespoons butter, diced, plus extra for greasing
1 cup lukewarm water
⅓ cup finely chopped candied pineapple
2 tablespoons finely chopped dried mango
1 cup unsweetened dried shredded coconut, toasted, plus extra for sprinkling
1 egg, lightly beaten

method

1 Grease a baking sheet. Sift together the flour, salt, and ginger into a large, warm bowl. Stir in the bran, yeast, and sugar. Rub in the butter with your fingertips until the mixture resembles bread crumbs. Add the water and mix to form a dough.

2 Invert the dough onto a lightly floured work surface and knead for 5–10 minutes, or until smooth and elastic. Put the dough in a greased bowl, cover with plastic wrap, and let rise in a warm place for 30 minutes, or until doubled in size.

3 Invert the dough again and knead in the pineapple, mango, and coconut. Shape into a circle and transfer to the prepared baking sheet. Score the top with the back of a knife. Cover with plastic wrap and let rest in a warm place for 30 minutes. Preheat the oven to 425°F.

4 Brush the loaf with the beaten egg and sprinkle with coconut. Bake in the preheated oven for 30 minutes, or until golden brown. Transfer to a wire rack to cool.

malted fruit loaf

ingredients

makes 1 loaf

2¾ cups all-purpose flour,
plus extra for dusting
1 teaspoon salt
1 teaspoon active dry yeast
1 cup golden raisins
1 cup lukewarm water
2 teaspoons vegetable oil,
plus extra for brushing
2 tablespoons malt extract
1½ tablespoons molasses

method

1 Sift together the flour and salt into a bowl and stir in the yeast and golden raisins. Make a well in the center and pour in the water, vegetable oil, malt extract, and molasses. Stir well with a wooden spoon until the dough begins to come together, then knead with your hands until it leaves the side of the bowl. Invert onto a lightly floured surface and knead well for about 10 minutes, or until smooth and elastic.

2 Brush a bowl with oil. Shape the dough into a ball, put it in the bowl, and cover. Let rise in a warm place for 1–2 hours, or until the dough has doubled in volume.

3 Brush a 9-inch loaf pan with oil. Invert the dough onto a lightly floured surface and knead for 1 minute. With lightly floured hands, flatten the dough into a rectangle the same width as the pan. Fold it into three and place in the prepared pan, seam-side down. Cover and let rise in a warm place for 30–40 minutes, or until the dough has reached the top of the pan.

4 Meanwhile, preheat the oven to 450°F. Bake the loaf for 30–40 minutes, or until it has shrunk from the side of the pan, the crust is golden brown, and it sounds hollow when tapped on the bottom with your knuckles. Invert onto a wire rack to cool.

spiced pumpkin bread

ingredients

makes 1 loaf

vegetable oil, for brushing
1 stick butter, softened,
    plus extra for greasing
½ cup sugar
2 eggs, lightly beaten
1 cup pumpkin puree
1¾ cups all-purpose flour
1½ teaspoons baking powder
½ teaspoon salt
1 teaspoon ground allspice
2 tablespoons pumpkin seeds

method

1 Preheat the oven to 400°F. Brush a 9-inch loaf pan with oil.

2 In a bowl, cream together the butter and sugar until light and fluffy. Add the beaten eggs, a little at a time. Stir in the pumpkin puree, then sift in the flour, baking powder, salt, and allspice.

3 Fold the pumpkin seeds gently through the batter in a figure-eight movement. Spoon the batter into the prepared loaf pan. Bake in the oven for about 1¼–1½ hours, or until a toothpick inserted into the center of the loaf comes out clean. Transfer to a wire rack to cool.

irish fruit bread

ingredients

makes 1 loaf

4³/₄ cups white bread flour,
   plus extra for dusting
1 teaspoon allspice
1 teaspoon salt
2 teaspoons active dry yeast
1 tablespoon sugar
1¹/₄ cups lukewarm milk
²/₃ cup lukewarm water
vegetable oil, for brushing
3¹/₂ tablespoons butter, softened,
   plus extra to serve
1¹/₂ cups mixed dried fruit, such as
   golden raisins, dried currants,
   and raisins
milk, for glazing

method

1 Sift the flour, allspice, and salt into a warm bowl. Stir in the yeast and sugar. Make a well in the center and pour in the milk and water. Mix well to make a sticky dough. Invert the dough onto a lightly floured work surface and knead until no longer sticky. Put the dough in an oiled bowl, cover with plastic wrap, and let rise in a warm place for 1 hour, or until doubled in size.

2 Invert the dough onto a floured work surface and knead lightly for 1 minute. Add the butter and dried fruit to the dough and work them in until completely incorporated. Return the dough to the bowl, cover, and let rise for 30 minutes.

3 Brush a 9-inch round cake pan with oil. Pat the dough into a neat circle and fit in the pan. Cover and let rest in a warm place until the dough has risen to the top of the pan. Meanwhile, preheat the oven to 400°F.

4 Brush the top of the loaf lightly with milk and bake in the preheated oven for 15 minutes. Cover with aluminum foil, reduce the oven temperature to 350°F, and bake for an additional 45 minutes, or until golden brown and it sounds hollow when tapped on the bottom. Transfer to a wire rack to cool. Serve with butter.

bran & yogurt bread

ingredients

makes 1 small loaf

1½ cups white bread flour,
    plus extra for dusting
1 cup whole-wheat bread flour
1 teaspoon salt
¾ teaspoon active dry yeast
½ cup wheat bran
⅔ cup lukewarm water
½ cup plain yogurt
1 tablespoon vegetable oil,
    plus extra for brushing
1 tablespoon molasses or
    light corn syrup

method

1 Sift together both flours and the salt into a bowl and tip in the bran from the sifter. Stir in the yeast and wheat bran. Make a well in the center and pour in the water, yogurt, oil, and molasses. Stir well with a wooden spoon until the dough begins to come together, then knead with your hands until it leaves the side of the bowl. Invert onto a lightly floured surface and knead well for about 10 minutes, or until smooth and elastic.

2 Brush a bowl with oil. Shape the dough into a ball, put it in the bowl, and cover. Let rise in a warm place for 1–2 hours, or until the dough has doubled in size.

3 Brush a baking sheet with oil. Invert the dough onto a lightly floured surface, punch down with your fist to knock out the air, and knead for 1 minute. With lightly floured hands, shape the dough into a ball and flatten slightly. Put the loaf onto the prepared baking sheet, cover, and let rise in a warm place for 30 minutes.

4 Preheat the oven to 425°F. Slash the top of the loaf and bake for 30 minutes, or until golden brown and it sounds hollow when tapped on the bottom with your knuckles. Transfer to a wire rack to cool.

muesli bread

ingredients

makes 1 loaf

2¼ cups white bread flour,
    plus extra for dusting
⅔ cup whole-wheat bread flour
1½ teaspoons salt
1¾ cups unsweetened muesli
3 tablespoons instant nonfat
    dry milk
1 envelope active dry yeast
1 cup lukewarm water
2 tablespoons vegetable oil,
    plus extra for brushing
1 tablespoon honey
½ cup chopped dried apricots

method

1 Sift together the flours and salt into a bowl and tip in
the bran from the sifter. Stir in the muesli, instant dry
milk, and yeast. Make a well in the center and pour
in the water, oil, and honey. Stir well until the dough
begins to come together, then knead until it leaves the
side of the bowl. Invert onto a lightly floured surface
and knead well for 5 minutes. Knead in the apricots
and continue to knead for an additional 5 minutes, or
until the dough is smooth and elastic.

2 Brush a bowl with oil. Shape the dough into a ball,
put it in the bowl, and cover. Let rise in a warm place
for 1 hour, or until doubled in size.

3 Brush a baking sheet with oil. Invert the dough onto a
lightly floured surface and knead briefly for 1 minute.
With lightly floured hands, shape the dough into a
circle and place on the prepared baking sheet. Cut
a cross in the top of the loaf. Cover and let rise in a
warm place for 30–40 minutes. Meanwhile, preheat
the oven to 400°F.

4 Bake the loaf for 30–35 minutes, or until firm and
golden brown. Transfer to a wire rack to cool.

lavender & honey spirals

ingredients

makes 9

3½ tablespoons butter, melted, plus extra for greasing
3¼ cups white bread flour, plus extra for dusting
1 teaspoon salt
1 envelope active dry yeast
1¼ cups lukewarm milk, plus extra for glazing
3 tablespoons lavender honey
1 tablespoon dried lavender flowers
1 tablespoon raw brown sugar

method

1 Grease a 9-inch round spring-form cake pan with butter. Place the flour and salt in a bowl and stir in the yeast. Make a well in the center and add the milk, 2 tablespoons of the honey, and 2 tablespoons of the butter, mixing to a soft dough.

2 Invert the dough onto a lightly floured surface and knead for about 10 minutes, until smooth, then return to the bowl, cover, and let rest for 5 minutes.

3 Invert the dough onto a lightly floured surface and lightly knead again. Roll out to a 10 x 12-inch rectangle. Brush with the remaining butter and sprinkle with the lavender flowers and sugar.

4 Firmly roll up the dough from one long edge, then cut into nine equal slices and arrange in the prepared pan, cut-side up.

5 Cover and let rest in a warm place for about 1 hour, or until the dough has doubled in size. Meanwhile, preheat the oven to 375°F.

6 Brush the spirals with milk and bake in the preheated oven for 30–35 minutes, or until golden brown. Warm the remaining honey and brush over the surface of the spirals, then remove from the pan and transfer to a wire rack to cool. Pull the spirals apart to serve.

chocolate bread

ingredients

makes 1 loaf

3¼ cups white bread flour,
    plus extra for dusting
1 teaspoon salt
¼ cup unsweetened cocoa powder
1 envelope active dry yeast
2 tablespoons packed light
    brown sugar
1 tablespoon oil, plus extra
    for brushing
1¼ cups lukewarm water
butter, for greasing and serving

method

1 Sift together the flour, salt, and cocoa powder into a large bowl. Stir in the yeast and sugar. Make a well in the center. Add the oil and water to the well and mix to form a dough.

2 Invert the dough onto a lightly floured work surface and knead for 5–10 minutes, or until smooth and elastic. Put the dough in an oiled bowl, cover, and let rise in a warm place for 1 hour, or until doubled in size. Lightly grease a 9-inch loaf pan.

3 Invert the dough again and knead lightly for 1 minute. Shape into a loaf. Transfer the dough to the prepared pan, cover, and let rest in a warm place for 30 minutes. Meanwhile, preheat the oven to 400°F.

4 Bake the loaf in the preheated oven for 25–30 minutes, or until it sounds hollow when tapped on the bottom. Transfer the loaf to a wire rack to cool. Serve with butter.

italian chocolate chip bread

ingredients

makes 1 loaf

vegetable oil, for brushing
1¾ cups all-purpose flour,
  plus extra for dusting
1 tablespoon unsweetened
  cocoa powder
pinch of salt
1 tablespoon butter, plus
  ½ teaspoon butter, melted,
  for brushing
1 tablespoon sugar
1 envelope active dry yeast
⅔ cup lukewarm water
⅓ cup semisweet chocolate chips

method

1 Brush a baking sheet with oil. Sift the flour, cocoa powder, and salt into a bowl. Add the butter and cut it into the dry ingredients until it forms crumbs, then stir in the sugar and yeast.

2 Gradually add the water, stirring well with a wooden spoon until the dough begins to come together, then knead with your hands until it leaves the side of the bowl. Invert onto a lightly floured surface and knead for about 10 minutes, or until smooth and elastic.

3 Knead the chocolate chips into the dough, then form into a round loaf. Put the loaf onto the prepared baking sheet and cover. Let rise in a warm place for 1–1½ hours, or until the dough has doubled in size. Preheat the oven to 425°F.

4 Bake the loaf in the preheated oven for 10 minutes, then reduce the oven temperature to 375°F and bake for an additional 15 minutes. Transfer the loaf to a wire rack and brush the top with the melted butter. Cover with a dish towel and let cool.

gluten-free recipes

buckwheat soda bread

ingredients

makes 1 loaf

1 cup buckwheat flour,
   plus extra for sprinkling
²/₃ cup rice flour
1 teaspoon salt
1 teaspoon xanthan gum
2 teaspoons gluten-free
   baking powder
1¼ cups milk, plus extra
   for glazing
1 teaspoon white wine vinegar
1 tablespoon olive oil

method

1 Preheat the oven to 400°F. Sift together the buckwheat flour, rice flour, salt, xanthan gum, and baking powder into a bowl and make a well in the center.

2 Mix together the milk, vinegar, and oil and stir into the dry ingredients to make a soft dough.

3 Sprinkle a little flour over a baking sheet. Shape the dough into a smooth 8-inch circle and place on the baking sheet. Lightly press to flatten, then use a sharp knife to cut a deep cross into the loaf.

4 Brush with milk to glaze and bake in the preheated oven for 25–30 minutes, or until risen, firm, and golden brown. Transfer to a wire rack to cool.

gluten-free flatbreads

ingredients

makes 4

1⅔ cups buckwheat flour, plus extra for dusting
⅔ cup rice flour
1 teaspoon salt
1 teaspoon gluten-free baking powder
½ teaspoon ground cumin
2 tablespoons chopped fresh cilantro
1 cup water
2 tablespoons olive oil

method

1 Sift together the buckwheat flour, rice flour, salt, baking powder, and cumin into a large bowl and make a well in the center.

2 Add the cilantro, water, and oil and stir into the dry ingredients to make a soft dough.

3 Divide the dough into four pieces and shape each piece into a smooth ball. Roll out each ball on a lightly floured surface to an 8-inch circle.

4 Preheat a ridged grill pan or barbecue to very hot. Add the flatbreads and cook for about 1 minute on each side, or until firm and golden brown. Serve warm.

soft corn tortillas

ingredients

makes 12

2 cups masa harina (ground
   cornmeal treated with lime)
¼ teaspoon salt
1¼ cups lukewarm water

method

1 Put the masa harina and salt into a bowl and make a
   well in the center. Stir in just enough of the water to
   mix to a moist, firm dough. Cover and let stand for
   15 minutes.

2 Divide the dough into 12 pieces, roll each piece into a
   smooth ball, then place between two sheets of plastic
   wrap and roll with a rolling pin (or use a tortilla press)
   to a thin 8-inch circle.

3 Heat a flat griddle pan or skillet until hot, place a tortilla
   on it, cook for about 20 seconds, then flip over. Cook
   for an additional 20 seconds, then turn once again and
   cook until it puffs slightly.

4 Remove from the pan, cover with a clean dish towel,
   and keep warm while cooking the remaining tortillas.
   Serve warm.

quick tomato focaccia

ingredients

makes 1 loaf

3 tablespoons olive oil, plus extra
    for brushing
1²/₃ cups buckwheat flour
1³/₄ cups potato flour
1¹/₄ cups rice flour
2 teaspoons xanthan gum
2¹/₄ teaspoons gluten-free
    fast-action yeast
1¹/₂ teaspoons salt
¹/₂ teaspoon black onion seeds
20 sun-dried tomato pieces,
    soaked, drained, and chopped
2¹/₂ cups lukewarm water
1 medium egg, beaten
2 garlic cloves, cut into slivers
few sprigs of fresh oregano

method

1 Brush a 13 x 9-inch baking pan with oil. Mix the flours, xanthan gum, yeast, salt, and onion seeds in a bowl and stir in the tomatoes.

2 Make a well in the center and stir in the water, egg, and 1 tablespoon of oil to make a soft dough. Beat the dough firmly, using a wooden spoon, for 4–5 minutes, then spoon in the baking pan, spreading evenly with a spatula.

3 Cover with oiled plastic wrap and let stand in a warm place for about 1 hour, or until doubled in size. Preheat the oven to 425°F.

4 Press pieces of garlic and oregano into the dough at intervals. Drizzle with the remaining oil, then bake in the preheated oven for 25–30 minutes, or until firm and golden brown. Invert and cool on a wire rack.

red pepper corn bread

ingredients

makes 1 loaf

1 large red bell pepper, seeded
    and sliced
1¼ cups cornmeal
1 cup gluten-free all-purpose flour
1 tablespoon gluten-free
    baking powder
1 teaspoon salt
2 teaspoons raw brown sugar
1 cup milk
2 eggs, lightly beaten
3 tablespoons olive oil,
    plus extra for brushing

method

1 Preheat the oven to 400°F. Arrange the red bell pepper slices on a baking sheet and roast in the preheated oven for 35 minutes, until tender and the skin begins to blister. Set aside to cool slightly, then peel away the skin.

2 Meanwhile, mix together the cornmeal, flour, baking powder, salt, and sugar in a large mixing bowl. Beat together the milk, eggs, and oil in a separate bowl and gradually add to the cornmeal mixture. Beat with a wooden spoon to make a thick, smooth, batter-like consistency.

3 Brush an 8½-inch loaf pan with oil. Finely chop the red pepper and fold into the cornmeal mixture, then spoon into the prepared pan. Bake in the preheated oven for 30 minutes, until lightly golden. Let rest in the pan for 10 minutes, then run a knife around the edge of the pan and invert the loaf onto a wire rack to cool.

zucchini & corn bread squares

ingredients

makes 9

vegetable oil, for brushing
1 cup cornmeal
1¼ cups soybean flour
1 tablespoon gluten-free
    baking powder
1 teaspoon salt
½ teaspoon pepper
1 zucchini, grated
1 extra-large egg, beaten
1¼ cups unsweetened soy milk
3 tablespoons olive oil

method

1 Preheat the oven to 375°F. Brush a shallow, 7½-inch square cake pan with oil.

2 Put the cornmeal, flour, baking powder, salt, and pepper into a bowl. Stir in the zucchini.

3 Beat together the egg, milk, and oil and stir into the dry ingredients, mixing evenly to a soft batter.

4 Spoon the batter into the prepared pan and smooth level with a spatula.

5 Bake in the preheated oven for 30–35 minutes, or until firm and golden brown. Let cool for 10 minutes in the pan, then cut into squares to serve.

swiss cheese & mustard slice

ingredients

makes 1 loaf

1 tablespoon olive oil,
    plus extra for brushing
1²/₃ cups buckwheat flour
1²/₃ cups potato flour
²/₃ cup rice flour
1½ teaspoons salt
2 teaspoons xanthan gum
1 envelope gluten-free,
    active dry yeast
1¼ cups lukewarm water
1 medium egg, beaten
2 tablespoons gluten-free
    whole-grain mustard
1 cup shredded swiss cheese

method

1 Brush a 13- x 9-inch baking pan with oil. Sift together the buckwheat flour, potato flour, rice flour, salt, and xanthan gum into a bowl, then stir in the yeast.

2 Make a well in the center and stir in the water, egg, and oil to make a soft dough. Beat with a wooden spoon for about 1 minute, or until smooth. Divide the dough into two pieces.

3 Brush a work surface with oil and roll out one piece of the dough. Use the rolling pin to lift it into the prepared pan, pressing out with your knuckles. Spread the dough with the mustard and sprinkle with about two-thirds of the cheese.

4 Roll out the remaining dough to cover the first piece, pressing with your fingers to make indentations in the dough. Cover and let rest in a warm place for about 1 hour, or until doubled in size. Meanwhile, preheat the oven to 425°F.

5 Sprinkle the remaining cheese over the dough and bake in the preheated oven for 25–30 minutes, or until firm and golden brown. Transfer to a wire rack to cool.

parmesan & garlic rolls

ingredients

makes 12

2 tablespoons olive oil,
 plus extra for brushing
3 garlic cloves, crushed
3 cups gluten-free flour blend,
 plus extra for dusting
1½ teaspoons salt
1 envelope gluten-free,
 active dry yeast
⅔ cup finely grated fresh
 Parmesan cheese
1¼ cups lukewarm water
milk, for glazing

method

1 Brush a baking sheet with oil. Heat the 2 tablespoons of oil in a saucepan, add the garlic, and gently stir-fry for about 1 minute, without browning. Remove from the heat and let cool slightly.

2 Sift together the flour and salt into a bowl, then stir in the yeast and three-quarters of the cheese. Make a well in the center and add the water and garlic oil, stirring to make a soft dough.

3 Invert the dough onto a lightly floured surface and lightly knead until smooth. Divide into 12 pieces and shape each piece into a smooth circle.

4 Place the circles on the prepared baking sheet and cut a deep cross into the top of each one with a sharp knife. Cover and let rest in a warm place for about 1 hour, or until doubled in size. Meanwhile, preheat the oven to 400°F.

5 Brush the tops of the rolls with milk and sprinkle with the remaining cheese. Bake in the preheated oven for 12–15 minutes, or until firm and golden brown. Transfer to a wire rack to cool.

quinoa & chive rolls

ingredients

makes 8

1 tablespoon olive oil,
plus extra for brushing
1²/₃ cups buckwheat flour
1¹/₃ cups potato flour
2 teaspoons xanthan gum
1¹/₂ teaspoons salt
1 envelope gluten-free,
active dry yeast
¹/₂ cup quinoa
3 tablespoons snipped chives
1¹/₂ cups lukewarm water
1 medium egg, beaten
milk, for glazing

method

1 Brush a large baking sheet with oil. Sift together the buckwheat flour, potato flour, xanthan gum, and salt into a bowl, then stir in the yeast, quinoa, and chives.

2 Make a well in the center and stir in the water, egg, and oil to make a soft dough. Lightly knead the dough until smooth.

3 Divide the dough into eight pieces and shape each piece into a smooth ball. Arrange on the prepared baking sheet, cover, and let rest in a warm place for about 1 hour, or until doubled in size. Meanwhile, preheat the oven to 400°F.

4 Brush the rolls with milk to glaze. Bake in the preheated oven for 20–25 minutes, or until firm and golden brown. Transfer to a wire rack to cool.

chicken & basil pizza

ingredients

makes 1 pizza

vegetable oil, for brushing
2¾ cups gluten-free flour blend
1 teaspoon salt
1 envelope gluten-free,
    active dry yeast
1 cup lukewarm water
2 tablespoons olive oil

topping

¾ cup chunky tomato sauce
1 red onion, thinly sliced
3 tablespoons chopped fresh basil,
    plus extra to garnish
1¼ cups diced, cooked chicken
4 ounces mozzarella cheese, diced
salt and pepper

method

1 Brush a large baking sheet with oil. Sift the flour and salt into a bowl and stir in the yeast. Make a well in the center, add the water with 1 tablespoon of the olive oil, and lightly mix to form a soft dough.

2 Lightly knead the dough to a smooth ball, then roll out to a 14-inch circle on the prepared baking sheet, pinching the edges slightly to make a raised edge. Cover and let rest in a warm place for 1–1½ hours, or until well risen and springy to the touch.

3 Preheat the oven to 400°F. Spread the tomato sauce over the dough to within ½ inch of the edge. Sprinkle with the onion, basil, and chicken, then top with the cheese. Season with salt and pepper, then sprinkle with the remaining oil.

4 Bake in the preheated oven for 25–30 minutes, or until firm and golden. Sprinkle with basil and serve hot.

shallot & bacon loaf

ingredients

makes 1 small loaf

vegetable oil, for brushing
1 tablespoon olive oil
2 shallots, thinly sliced
3 ounces bacon or pancetta,
    finely chopped
2 cups gluten-free flour blend
½ teaspoon salt
1 teaspoon gluten-free,
    active dry yeast
1 tablespoon maple syrup
1 cup lukewarm water

method

1 Brush an 8½-inch loaf pan with oil and line the bottom with nonstick parchment paper. Heat the olive oil in a skillet, then add the shallots and bacon and sauté for about 5 minutes, stirring occasionally, or until soft and golden. Remove from the heat and let cool slightly.

2 Mix the flour, salt, and yeast in a bowl and make a well in the center.

3 Mix together the maple syrup and water and stir into the dry ingredients with the shallots and bacon, lightly mixing to form a soft, sticky dough.

4 Spoon the dough into the prepared pan and spread evenly. Cover with oiled plastic wrap and let rest in a warm place for about 1 hour, or until the dough has risen and is spongy to the touch. Meanwhile, preheat the oven to 400°F.

5 Bake in the preheated oven for 30–35 minutes, or until golden brown and firm. Serve warm.

orange & mint rolls

ingredients

makes 12

1 tablespoon sunflower oil,
    plus extra for brushing
3 cups gluten-free flour blend, plus
    extra for dusting
1 teaspoon salt
1/3 cup firmly packed light
    brown sugar
1 envelope gluten-free,
    active dry yeast
1/2 teaspoon dried mint
finely grated rind of 1 orange
1/2 cup orange juice, plus extra
    for glazing
1 1/4 cups lukewarm water

method

1 Brush a large baking sheet with oil. Sift together the flour and salt into a bowl, then stir in the sugar, yeast, and mint. Make a well in the center and add the orange rind, orange juice, oil, and enough water to mix to a soft dough.

2 Invert the dough onto a lightly floured surface and lightly knead until smooth. Divide into 12 pieces, shape each piece into a circle, and place on the prepared baking sheet.

3 Lightly press the circles to flatten, then cut three slashes across the top of each roll with a sharp knife. Cover with oiled plastic wrap and let rest in a warm place for about 1 hour, or until well risen. Meanwhile, preheat the oven to 400°F.

4 Brush the rolls with orange juice to glaze. Bake in the preheated oven for 12–15 minutes, or until golden brown and firm. Transfer to a wire rack to cool.

cinnamon & cranberry bread

ingredients

makes 1 loaf

oil, for brushing
1¾ cups gluten-free flour blend, plus extra for dusting
⅓ cup firmly packed light brown sugar
1½ teaspoons ground cinnamon
1 envelope gluten-free, active dry yeast
⅓ cup dried cranberries
1 cup lukewarm cranberry juice
1 egg, beaten
2 tablespoons butter, melted

method

1 Brush a baking sheet with oil. Sift together the flour, sugar, and cinnamon into a bowl and stir in the yeast and cranberries.

2 Make a well in the center and stir in the cranberry juice, egg, and butter to make a soft dough. Beat with a wooden spoon for 2 minutes.

3 Invert onto a lightly floured surface and shape the dough into a 12-inch-long roll. Place on the prepared baking sheet, cover with oiled plastic wrap, and let rest in a warm place for about 1 hour, or until doubled in size. Meanwhile, preheat the oven to 400°F.

4 Bake the loaf in the preheated oven for 35–40 minutes, or until firm and golden brown. Transfer to a wire rack to cool.

gluten-free hot cross buns

ingredients

makes 12

vegetable oil, for brushing
3½ cups gluten-free flour blend
1 teaspoon salt
2 teaspoons allspice
1 envelope gluten-free,
   active dry yeast
2 extra-large eggs, beaten
2 tablespoons butter, melted
¼ cup honey
3–4 teaspoons lemon juice
1 cup mixed dried fruit
1⅓ cups lukewarm milk
⅔ cup confectioners' sugar

method

1 Brush a large baking sheet with oil. Sift the flour, salt, and allspice into a bowl and stir in the yeast.

2 Make a well in the center and add the eggs, butter, honey, 1 teaspoon of the lemon juice, and the dried fruit, with enough milk to mix to a soft, sticky dough.

3 Place 12 large, smooth spoonfuls of the dough on the prepared baking sheet (a large ice-cream scoop is useful). Cover with oiled plastic wrap and let rest in a warm place for 1–1½ hours, or until well risen and puffy. Meanwhile, preheat the oven to 425°F.

4 Bake in the preheated oven for 15–20 minutes, or until firm and golden brown. Transfer to a wire rack to cool.

5 Mix the confectioners' sugar with enough of the remaining lemon juice to make a thick paste, then spoon or pipe the paste on top of each bun to make a cross.

sweet almond & apricot loaf

ingredients

makes 1 loaf

1 tablespoon sunflower oil,
   plus extra for brushing
1¾ cups gluten-free flour blend
½ cup sugar
1 envelope gluten-free,
   active dry yeast
¾ cup almond meal
   (ground almonds)
1 cup chopped dried apricots
2 eggs, beaten
1¼ cups lukewarm milk
1 tablespoon slivered almonds

method

1 Brush a 9-inch loaf pan with oil and line the bottom with nonstick parchment paper. Sift together the flour, sugar, and yeast into a bowl and stir in the almond meal and apricots.

2 Make a well in the center and stir in the eggs, milk, and oil to make a soft, sticky dough. Beat with a wooden spoon for 2 minutes. Spoon the dough into the prepared pan, spreading evenly with a spatula.

3 Cover with oiled plastic wrap and let rest in a warm place for about 1 hour, or until well risen and springy to the touch. Meanwhile, preheat the oven to 400°F.

4 Sprinkle with the slivered almonds, then bake the loaf in the preheated oven for 30–35 minutes, or until firm and golden brown. Invert and transfer to a wire rack to cool.

banana & brazil nut loaf

ingredients

makes 1 loaf

¼ cup sunflower oil, plus extra for brushing

⅓ cup soybean flour

½ cup gluten-free cornstarch

½ cup tapioca (cassava) flour

2 teaspoons gluten-free baking powder

½ teaspoon xanthan gum

2 teaspoons allspice

⅓ cup firmly packed light brown sugar

2 eggs, beaten

1 teaspoon vanilla extract

3 ripe bananas, mashed

¾ cup brazil nuts, chopped

method

1 Brush a 9-inch loaf pan with oil and line it with parchment paper. Preheat the oven to 350°F.

2 Sift together the soybean flour, cornstarch, tapioca flour, baking powder, xanthan gum, and allspice into a bowl and add the sugar, eggs, vanilla extract, oil, and bananas. Beat well with a wooden spoon or an electric mixer until a thick batter forms.

3 Fold in the chopped nuts and spoon the batter into the prepared pan. Bake the loaf in the preheated oven for 45–50 minutes, or until golden brown and firm.

4 Let cool in the pan for 10 minutes, then invert and transfer to a wire rack to cool completely.

index